J.-K. Huysmans

Titles in the series Critical Lives present the work of leading cultural figures of the modern period. Each book explores the life of the artist, writer, philosopher or architect in question and relates it to their major works.

In the same series

Hannah Arendt *Samantha Rose Hill*
Antonin Artaud *David A. Shafer*
John Ashbery *Jess Cotton*
Roland Barthes *Andy Stafford*
Georges Bataille *Stuart Kendall*
Charles Baudelaire *Rosemary Lloyd*
Simone de Beauvoir *Ursula Tidd*
Samuel Beckett *Andrew Gibson*
Walter Benjamin *Esther Leslie*
John Berger *Andy Merrifield*
Leonard Bernstein *Paul R. Laird*
Joseph Beuys *Claudia Mesch*
Jorge Luis Borges *Jason Wilson*
Constantin Brancusi *Sanda Miller*
Bertolt Brecht *Philip Glahn*
Charles Bukowski *David Stephen Calonne*
Mikhail Bulgakov *J.A.E. Curtis*
William S. Burroughs *Phil Baker*
Byron *David Ellis*
John Cage *Rob Haskins*
Albert Camus *Edward J. Hughes*
Fidel Castro *Nick Caistor*
Paul Cézanne *Jon Kear*
Coco Chanel *Linda Simon*
Noam Chomsky *Wolfgang B. Sperlich*
Jean Cocteau *James S. Williams*
Joseph Conrad *Robert Hampson*
H.D. (Hilda Doolittle) *Lara Vetter*
Salvador Dalí *Mary Ann Caws*
Charles Darwin *J. David Archibald*
Guy Debord *Andy Merrifield*
Claude Debussy *David J. Code*
Gilles Deleuze *Frida Beckman*
Fyodor Dostoevsky *Robert Bird*
Marcel Duchamp *Caroline Cros*
Sergei Eisenstein *Mike O'Mahony*
Frantz Fanon *James Williams*
William Faulkner *Kirk Curnutt*
Gustave Flaubert *Anne Green*
Ford Madox Ford *Max Saunders*
Michel Foucault *David Macey*
Benjamin Franklin *Kevin J. Hayes*
Sigmund Freud *Matthew ffytche*
Mahatma Gandhi *Douglas Allen*
Antoni Gaudí *Michael Eaude*
Jean Genet *Stephen Barber*
Allen Ginsberg *Steve Finbow*
Johann Wolfgang von Goethe *Jeremy Adler*
Günter Grass *Julian Preece*
Ernest Hemingway *Verna Kale*
Langston Hughes *W. Jason Miller*
Victor Hugo *Bradley Stephens*
Zora Neale Hurston *Cheryl R. Hopson*
Aldous Huxley *Jake Poller*
J.-K. Huysmans *Ruth Antosh*
Derek Jarman *Michael Charlesworth*
Alfred Jarry *Jill Fell*
James Joyce *Andrew Gibson*

Carl Jung *Paul Bishop*
Franz Kafka *Sander L. Gilman*
Frida Kahlo *Gannit Ankori*
Søren Kierkegaard *Alastair Hannay*
Yves Klein *Nuit Banai*
Arthur Koestler *Edward Saunders*
Akira Kurosawa *Peter Wild*
Lenin *Lars T. Lih*
Jack London *Kenneth K. Brandt*
Pierre Loti *Richard M. Berrong*
Rosa Luxemburg *Dana Mills*
Jean-François Lyotard *Kiff Bamford*
René Magritte *Patricia Allmer*
Stéphane Mallarmé *Roger Pearson*
Thomas Mann *Herbert Lehnert and Eva Wessell*
Gabriel García Márquez *Stephen M. Hart*
Karl Marx *Paul Thomas*
Henri Matisse *Kathryn Brown*
Guy de Maupassant *Christopher Lloyd*
Herman Melville *Kevin J. Hayes*
Henry Miller *David Stephen Calonne*
Yukio Mishima *Damian Flanagan*
Eadweard Muybridge *Marta Braun*
Vladimir Nabokov *Barbara Wyllie*
Pablo Neruda *Dominic Moran*
Friedrich Nietzsche *Ritchie Robertson*
Georgia O'Keeffe *Nancy J. Scott*
Richard Owen *Patrick Armstrong*
Octavio Paz *Nick Caistor*
Pablo Picasso *Mary Ann Caws*
Edgar Allan Poe *Kevin J. Hayes*
Ezra Pound *Alec Marsh*
Marcel Proust *Adam Watt*
Sergei Rachmaninoff *Rebecca Mitchell*
Arthur Rimbaud *Seth Whidden*
John Ruskin *Andrew Ballantyne*
Jean-Paul Sartre *Andrew Leak*
Erik Satie *Mary E. Davis*
Arnold Schoenberg *Mark Berry*
Arthur Schopenhauer *Peter B. Lewis*
Dmitry Shostakovich *Pauline Fairclough*
Adam Smith *Jonathan Conlin*
Susan Sontag *Jerome Boyd Maunsell*
Gertrude Stein *Lucy Daniel*
Stendhal *Francesco Manzini*
Igor Stravinsky *Jonathan Cross*
Rabindranath Tagore *Bashabi Fraser*
Pyotr Tchaikovsky *Philip Ross Bullock*
Leo Tolstoy *Andrei Zorin*
Leon Trotsky *Paul Le Blanc*
Mark Twain *Kevin J. Hayes*
Richard Wagner *Raymond Furness*
Alfred Russel Wallace *Patrick Armstrong*
Simone Weil *Palle Yourgrau*
Tennessee Williams *Paul Ibell*
Ludwig Wittgenstein *Edward Kanterian*
Virginia Woolf *Ira Nadel*
Frank Lloyd Wright *Robert McCarter*

J.-K. Huysmans

Ruth Antosh

REAKTION BOOKS

For my husband, John Antosh

Published by Reaktion Books Ltd
Unit 32, Waterside
44–48, Wharf Road
London N1 7UX, UK
www.reaktionbooks.co.uk

First published 2024
Copyright © Ruth Antosh 2024

Printed and bound in Great Britain by Bell & Bain, Glasgow

A catalogue record for this book is available from the British Library

ISBN 978 1 78914 872 5

Contents

1 Beginnings 7

2 Under the Influence of Zola and Naturalism 27

3 *À rebours* and Beyond 41

4 Descending into Darkness: *Là-bas*, the Abbé Boullan
and the Occult 61

5 The Spiritual Journey Begins: Religious Retreats and
Huysmans' Conversion 78

6 In Search of a Monastery: The Road to Ligugé 91

7 The Final Years 119

Epilogue 138

References 143

Bibliography 153

Acknowledgements 157

Photo Acknowledgements 159

Huysmans at his desk, photographed by Frédéric Boissonnas and André Taponier, *c*. 1900.

1

Beginnings

J.-K. Huysmans occupies a significant place in French literature, both as an advocate of naturalism and, paradoxically, as a rebel against it. Although best known for his groundbreaking novel *À rebours*, in which a solitary protagonist withdraws from reality into a world of artifice and dream, Huysmans wrote many other remarkable novels, and he was a perceptive and talented art critic who was among the first to recognize the genius of Degas and the Impressionists. He attracted readers over the years, not only because of his writings, but because of his personal life, which he spent in a quest for spiritual and aesthetic satisfaction. Huysmans' spiritual journey appeals to all who are dissatisfied with life and long for some better existence. In his writings, Huysmans describes an indefinable longing, whether it be for a better meal, a more comfortable home, an ideal lover or a more perfect world beyond everyday reality.

There are few nineteenth-century writers whose fiction and personal life are so closely intertwined; it has become a commonplace to assume that most, if not all, of Huysmans' protagonists are versions of the author himself. And, indeed, there are often striking similarities. Yet this tendency to assume a correlation between Huysmans' fiction and his life is fraught with pitfalls. Because there is very little available information about his childhood and adolescence, biographers have tended to mine his novels for descriptions of the protagonists' youth and then present the information as factual. The most highly regarded biography of Huysmans, *The Life of J.-K. Huysmans* by Robert Baldick, frequently takes this approach, and most subsequent scholars have to one degree or another followed suit.[1] A few have voiced concerns that this may lead to false assumptions. Christopher Lloyd, for instance, remarks that critics who equate Durtal, the hero of Huysmans' last four novels, with the author himself 'seem to be making a somewhat facile and ingenuous identification between biographical and fictional, with the result that our perspectives on both are blurred rather than sharpened'.[2] The present study seeks to avoid excessive reliance on Huysmans' fiction as a source of biographical details. We will try, in the absence of documented information, to present plausible assumptions based on what is known about the author and his times.

Surprisingly little information exists concerning Huysmans' childhood and adolescence. Was his boyhood happy or miserable? Did his mother lavish him with affection or neglect him after his father died? Huysmans wrote virtually nothing about his own childhood, probably because of a wish to keep his personal life separate from his public image. What little information we do have is based largely on bureaucratic documents and a few stray comments he made in some of his non-fiction writings. He seems not even to have discussed his youth with close friends, a fact that may be explained by his natural reticence.

The facts as they are known are as follows: Huysmans was born in Paris on 5 February 1848 at 11 rue Suger (now no. 9). His young mother, Élisabeth-Malvina Badin Huysmans, had been a schoolteacher before she married, and his father, Victor-Godfried-Jan Huysmans, was a Dutch immigrant who worked in Paris as a commercial artist. Victor-Godfried came from a long line of successful Dutch painters, dating back to the sixteenth century, notably Cornelius Huysmans (1648–1727); nine landscapes attributed to him or his workshop are now in the Louvre. The boy was christened Charles-Marie-Georges and baptized at the nearby church of Saint-Séverin, a church Huysmans was to write about many years later. It was only when he wrote his first work of fiction that he began to use the Dutch form of his name: Joris-Karl, and even then he continued to use his baptismal name for all official documents.

Plaque at 9 rue Suger noting Huysmans' date of birth of 5 February 1848.

While Georges was still very young, his parents moved to 38 rue Saint-Sulpice. This was another church that later would play an important role in his fiction. The street was quiet. The boy would have been able to hear the church bells. The family's life was uneventful, except for occasional summer trips to visit Godfried's family in the Netherlands, where his older brother Constant was head of the Arts Academy in Breda, and several aunts were cloistered nuns. Huysmans' mother and father were not particularly devout, and according to Huysmans, his only religious education as a young child consisted of Dutch prayers his grandmother taught him during the family's visits to the Netherlands: 'My youth was not pious. In my early years I learned only a few Dutch prayers that my grandmother taught me to babble, and I didn't know them well.'[3]

In 1856 Godfried's health began to fail, and in June of that year he died. Huysmans was only eight years old. Though Huysmans never wrote anything about his father, he cherished several pictures by Godfried: a portrait of Huysmans' mother, a copy of Zurburán's *The Monk* and a self-portrait.

The question of Huysmans' relationship with his mother is more complex, though he never wrote anything about her, either. After her husband's death Malvina and Georges moved in with her parents at 11 rue de Sèvres, and she took a job in a department store. She sent young Georges off to boarding school nearby at the Institution Hortus, on the rue du Bac. Less than a year after her husband's death, she married a young man named Jules Og, of whom little is known except that he was a Protestant. He must have had some money, because he and Malvina purchased a bookbindery on the ground floor of the building where they lived on rue de Sèvres. In the ensuing years Jules and Malvina had two daughters, Blanche and Juliette.

Although there is no information suggesting that Georges disliked his stepfather, it has generally been assumed by biographers that the boy was deeply resentful of M. Og, and that he felt abandoned by his mother when she married and sent him to boarding school. Baldick states flatly that 'Malvina's speedy remarriage seemed to him a betrayal, M. Og a usurper.'[4] Some biographers have likened Huysmans to Baudelaire, arguing that just as Baudelaire despised M. Aupick, so young Georges loathed M. Og. Some have even claimed it was M. Og who had him sent away to school, and that he was seldom allowed to come home, spending most of his holidays and Sundays by himself at school. Yet not one shred of evidence exists to support this melodramatic interpretation, other than a short passage in one of his novels, *En ménage* (Living Together).

The truth is that Huysmans became a student at the Institution Hortus well *before* his mother remarried. There was nothing unusual about this: it was the custom of bourgeois families who wished their sons to become 'notables' to send them away to school. It was thought that boarding school sheltered them from the outside world, so that they could focus on their studies. While it is true that in *En ménage* the protagonist describes his unhappy experiences at boarding school, for instance the disgusting food and the freezing cold dormitories, there is no proof that this is a completely factual account of Huysmans' own experiences at

Artist unknown (possibly Huysmans' father), sketch of Huysmans, aged eight.

Hortus. Research on the Institution Hortus has yielded evidence that Hortus was a well-run, highly respected school, winning praise from inspectors for its excellent facilities and curriculum. This is a far cry from the grim, forbidding place Huysmans' character describes in *En ménage*. While he may not have been particularly happy at Hortus, he made several lifelong friends while there. It is unlikely that he spent holidays at the school, like André in *En ménage*, since the family apartment was nearby.

In 1862 Huysmans left the Institution Hortus and entered the Lycée Saint-Louis as a scholarship student. The Lycée Saint-Louis still exists today and boasts many distinguished alumni, including Charles Gounod, Louis Pasteur, Charles Baudelaire and Émile Zola. Since scholarships at this time rarely covered more than a portion of a student's expenses, his family must have contributed a sizeable part of the tuition. Huysmans' mother and stepfather were people of modest means, and this surely involved sacrifices on their part. At the Lycée Saint-Louis he studied Latin, geography, history, Greek and French, as well as science and mathematics. Though he did not excel in mathematics or science, he won prizes each year in Latin, history, geography and, occasionally, Greek and French. He was particularly strong in Latin and once told a teacher that he worked on it by reading dual-language editions of Latin writers 'like the newspaper' in his spare time, checking the French translation for words he did not know. Huysmans pursued his studies at the Lycée Saint-Louis for three years, until 1865, when, at the age of seventeen, he adamantly refused to return there for his final year, telling his mother that he 'absolutely refused to return to any school, or lycée, or pension Hortus'.[5]

We do not know why he balked at completing his lycée studies, but one possibility is that, like his protagonist André Jayant in *En ménage*, he was being bullied by some of the wealthier boys, who looked down on him because his family was poor. But it also seems plausible that, like many bright young men of his era, he was simply tired of the dull routine of school. Nineteenth-century lycées were not especially exciting places; students endured strict discipline, long hours of study and had few opportunities for recreation. Rote memorization and translation of Latin and Greek texts were key aspects of the curriculum, and creativity was not encouraged. Georges was beginning to try his hand at writing poetry in French, and was developing a taste for Baudelaire, Balzac and Théophile Gautier, who were definitely not on the Lycée Saint-Louis' curriculum. He may have felt that in order to hone his skills in writing French, the best approach would be to work on his own, and that the strict schedule of study at the lycée was impeding his progress. The French language received short shrift in most nineteenth-century French lycées. At the time, only one hour per week was spent on French, while eight hours per week were devoted to Latin and Greek. French authors studied were primarily those of the seventeenth century, including Racine, Corneille and Molière. Students had no opportunity to read modern French authors.

Huysmans' mother was understandably upset at her son's wish to leave the lycée. When she asked how on earth he thought he would be able to pass the baccalaureate exam if he stopped attending school, Georges replied that he would study for it at home, on his own. Mother and son finally reached a compromise: he could quit the lycée, but he had to agree to take private lessons from one of the teachers at Saint-Louis. The tutor, M. Delzons, assured Mme Og that if her son was strong in Latin – the most important subject – he was almost certain to pass the baccalaureate. When Delzons gave the boy a difficult passage in Latin to translate as a way of gauging his proficiency in the language, Huysmans translated it in half an hour, without using a dictionary, making only two mistakes.[6]

The tutor's prediction was accurate, for on 7 March 1866, Georges passed the baccalaureate. Seeing that he had no idea what he wanted to do in life, and fearing that he would get into trouble if he did not have plenty of work to keep him busy, his mother and stepfather encouraged him to follow the Badin family tradition and become a civil servant. (His grandfather and uncle had both worked at the Ministry of the Interior.) It is likely that his parents hoped these family connections with the Ministry would help him get hired there. Huysmans seems to have had no objections to this plan. He wrote a letter of application to the Ministry of the Interior, was accepted as an *employé de sixième classe* (a grand title that meant a filing clerk) and began work there in April 1866. He was only eighteen. His family pressed him to enrol in law school part time, and so, in the autumn of the same year, while continuing his job at the Ministry of the Interior, he began studying law at the University of Paris.

While Georges was not openly disobedient, he had a mind of his own and soon decided that he could not bear the boredom of law school, even though he passed the first exam with a decent score. The material was dry and dull, and he later recalled 'the disgust I felt while poring over sad, useless legal cases'.[7]

In 1867 he abandoned his law studies. Besides ignoring his parents' wishes that he plan on a legal career, Huysmans further asserted his independence by moving out of the family residence at 11 rue de Sèvres and into his own apartment. From this point on, he began to enjoy the vibrant night life of the Latin Quarter after finishing his work each day. He now had time to work on his own writing, and a regular (though modest) salary to pay his living expenses. This comfortable lifestyle was to continue for decades.

When Georges dropped out of law school, his mother was surely disappointed, as she had been when he decided not to return to the lycée, since a degree in law would have enabled her son to pursue a more lucrative career. However, she accepted his decision. She was now a widow; her husband, Huysmans'

Huysmans at home, 11 rue de Sèvres, Paris.

stepfather, M. Og, had died that same year, and she had two young daughters to raise. Georges was now the man of the family with a job and his own apartment, and although she had always taken a keen interest in her son's education and career plans, no doubt she felt that he had a right to make his own decisions.

Huysmans' closest friend during this period of new-found independence was Ludovic de Vente de Francmesnil, a fellow civil servant who worked at the Ministry of War. Their friendship began at law school, where, coincidentally, they shared the same tutor. The two had similar tastes in art, literature and night life, and on weekends they began taking long walks through Paris's working-class neighbourhoods along the Bièvre. Occasionally they would stop at a down-at-heel bistro to have a drink and surreptitiously observe the Parisian *ouvriers*. Sometimes they would even attend a dance at a tavern in a grimy suburb, or drop in at a café concert to watch the crowd and enjoy the ambience of raucous *joie de vivre*. On Sundays the two friends would often spend hours at the Louvre, where they particularly admired the old Dutch masters, especially Rembrandt, Teniers and Jordaens. They also began to frequent a rather unimpressive little theatre in the Latin Quarter called the Bobino. Here they would gawk at the pretty but not very talented actresses while enjoying a good cigar.

In the summer of 1867 Huysmans visited the Exposition Universelle or World's Fair in Paris, at the Champ de Mars. Impressed by an exhibition of contemporary landscape painters that he saw there, and perhaps with Ludo's encouragement, he wrote a brief article about the exhibition and submitted it to an obscure magazine called *La Revue mensuelle*. The editor, Jean-Louis Le Hir, liked the piece, and in November 1867 Huysmans' article was published. His career as a writer had begun. The article is short and not especially impressive, but already one sees Huysmans' original tastes in art beginning to emerge. Although he had no formal education in art or art history, he had a perceptive eye for painterly technique. In the article he is especially interested in how artists convey the effects of light and colour; a painter's subject-matter is of far less importance to him than technique. While the article begins by praising the Dutch painters who exhibited at the Exposition, it moves on to focus on two contemporary French landscape artists: Meissonier and Diaz. Before discussing these painters, Huysmans expresses his profound admiration for Rembrandt. Although at the time Rembrandt was not generally recognized as the greatest Dutch master, Huysmans' unerring instinct is to view the artist as a genius. It seems clear that he had read fairly widely in the field of art criticism, especially Baudelaire and the Goncourts, and he had learned a great deal from visits to the Louvre with Ludo.

In December 1867 Huysmans published a second article in the *Revue mensuelle.* This time, it was not art criticism but a review of a play at the Bobino. It is little more than a brief listing of the actors and actresses, with a few words of praise for the production, but because in his novel *Marthe* a young man writes a review of a play in order to gain access to the pretty actress who has the main role, it is possible that one of the actresses mentioned was Huysmans' mistress, though the article does not reveal her name.

At age nineteen, Huysmans was now a published writer, though he remained virtually unknown. He might well have continued writing art and theatre reviews for the *Revue mensuelle*, but the journal went bankrupt and disappeared soon after his second article came into print. Following the publication of these two short articles, Huysmans began spending more and more of his spare time with others who shared his passion for art and literature. Like so many young intellectuals of his era, he met with friends in the cafes and cabarets of the Latin Quarter for heated literary discussions, and he read contemporary French poetry and novels: Baudelaire, Balzac, George Sand and Gautier were among his favourites. While enjoying his independence and working on fiction and prose poems, he was also savouring the company of the opposite sex. Besides some short affairs with working-class women, he was a frequent visitor to brothels. While patronizing brothels, he also began an affair with a young seamstress, Anna Meunier, who was to become his long-time companion.

This agreeable existence as a civil servant by day and a bohemian habitué of the cafes and theatres of the Latin Quarter by night came to an abrupt halt when France declared war against Prussia in 1869. In late July of that year, he was called up to serve in the Garde Nationale, 6th Battalion, which was about to leave for the front. His battalion was, like most of the French army, inadequately clothed and armed. In Châlons he had to stand guard using a wooden piquet instead of a rifle, and he watched angry soldiers jeer General Canrobert because they were hungry and poorly equipped.[8]

There is no indication that Huysmans felt a patriotic urge to fight for his country – especially in an ill-advised war against Prussia, a country for which he felt some affinity. He was a soldier purely because he had no choice in the matter. Before he could be sent to the front, however, Huysmans contracted dysentery and was sent to a military hospital at Châlons for treatment. While he was awaiting medical care, word arrived that the Prussians were marching towards Châlons. He and other sick soldiers were loaded chaotically onto a train bound for Evreux, farther from the invading Prussian forces. Along the way, Huysmans and a fellow soldier he had met at Châlons got off to look around when the train made a temporary stop at Arras, and upon returning to the station they found the train had left without them. The two young men managed to find their own way to the hospital in Evreux the next day, but Huysmans was directed to a nearby lycée, which had been converted into a temporary clinic. The lycée was a former monastery and still retained the atmosphere of a spiritual retreat, with religious verses written on the walls. It was here that Huysmans was cared for by a pretty young nun who left a lasting impression on him. Sœur Angèle in his short story 'Sac au dos' (Knapsack) was likely modelled after her.

Huysmans longed to go back to Paris, for there was little to do as he convalesced at the clinic. One day he happened to notice a familiar name in the local newspaper: that of M. Chefdeville, a notary and friend of Huysmans' family. He sent the man a letter, begging him to use his influence with the commanding general in Evreux so that he could get permission to visit his family in Paris. The obliging M. Chefdeville contacted the general, and after bidding farewell to the pretty young nun, Huysmans was on his way home to Paris, on sick leave.

Emperor Napoleon III had just suffered a decisive defeat at Sédan as Huysmans arrived in Paris in early September 1870. Just in the nick of time, he was able to enter the city before it was besieged by the Prussians. After visiting his mother, he returned to his own apartment, where nothing had changed, and all the furnishings and art objects seemed to welcome him home. He was still an enlisted man, and so when his sick leave ended on 10 November 1870 he was sent to work in the War Ministry, as 'sous secrétaire d'état major, remplissant la fonction de commis aux écritures', or invoicing clerk. The Prussian troops were bombarding the city. He saw and heard shells falling, and even collected the fragments of one shell to use as an ashtray. After Paris surrendered in February 1871, the seat of government was moved to Versailles and Huysmans was transferred there, where he resumed his old civilian job at the Ministry of the Interior. For a period of several months he did not leave Versailles, and when he finally travelled to Paris he was shocked by the devastation caused by heavy Prussian bombardment.

In 1871, after France's capitulation to the Prussians, Huysmans returned to Paris and continued to work at the Ministry of the Interior. He had a new apartment now on the rue du Cherche-Midi. He and Ludo resumed their walks around Paris and their visits to theatres, cafes and the Louvre. The two friends began meeting on Wednesday nights at Huysmans' apartment to discuss art and literature. Often they would discuss Huysmans' own efforts at writing, and in 1873 he showed Ludo the manuscript of a collection of Baudelairean prose poems entitled *Le Drageoir aux épices* (A Dish of Spices). It was an assortment of rather bizarre pieces, on such disparate subjects as death personified as a woman covered with ghastly red sores; a smoked herring; a festive gathering of peasants in a tavern (based on a picture by Jordaens); and a red-garbed femme fatale in a luxurious crimson room. Ludo, a connoisseur of poetry and fiction, realized that this work showed remarkable talent and urged his friend to seek out a publisher. After approaching several publishing houses, all of which turned it down, Huysmans asked his mother for advice. Apparently she supported his efforts to become a published author, for she contacted a publisher whom she knew through her bookbindery, Pierre-Jules Hetzel, asking him to take a look at the manuscript. Hetzel, a staid author of children's books, was taken aback by what he read, for some of the poems seemed indecent. He invited young Georges to come and talk over the work, and when Huysmans arrived, Hetzel was blunt in his criticism. He told the young author 'that he had no talent whatsoever, that he never would have any talent (and) that he wrote in an execrable style',[9]

Besides the humiliation of such a harsh verdict, Huysmans had to cope with his mother's dismay, since she had great faith in Hetzel's judgement. One can imagine that she urged her son to pursue a more practical path in life, and to return to law school. Discouraged and defeated, Huysmans likely considered abandoning his efforts to publish the manuscript and perhaps even thought of giving up writing, but Ludo would not hear of it. Convinced of the literary value of the *Le Drageoir aux épices*, Ludo approached his brother-in-law, M. Gratiot, a paper merchant with contacts in the literary world. M. Gratiot recommended the manuscript to Arsène Houssaye, the editor and owner of *La Revue du xixe siècle*, a highly regarded literary magazine. Impressed, Houssaye published extracts of the *Drageoir*. Despite the favourable critical reception, no publisher seemed interested in bringing the entire book into print, so Huysmans arranged to publish it at his own expense with the editor Dentu. The first edition of *Le Drageoir aux épices* appeared in 1874.[10] It is thought that Ludo helped finance the publication.

The Wednesday night gatherings at Huysmans' apartment continued, and before long Ludo brought two of his colleagues from the Ministry of War to join in: a quirky bibliophile named Jean-Jules-Athanase Bobin, nicknamed 'le professeur' because of his pedantic manner, and Henry Céard, a young aspiring writer.

'Le professeur' was an avid collector of original editions of sixteenth-century French authors, and Céard was writing prose poems, as was Huysmans. During animated discussions, the young men read aloud to each other from books they loved – both ancient and modern. Gustave Flaubert and the Goncourts were particular favourites. A year later, in 1875, Zola became their passion. They also admired medieval and Renaissance writers such as François Villon and Marguerite de Navarre. The friends talked about authors they despised as well: Victor Hugo was the most frequent object of their ridicule, though Huysmans secretly admired the chapter of *Les Misérables* in which the convent of the Petit-Picpus is described. These young men, well educated at privileged boarding schools and familiar with ancient Greek and Latin writers as well as contemporary French authors, were enamoured of art and literature. Gradually, Huysmans began reading some of his own work to them. Although his earliest attempts at fiction, including an ambitious project for a novel about a nineteen-year-old girl's experiences during the Prussian siege of Paris, have unfortunately been lost, he also wrote a sort of fictionalized memoir about his experiences during the Franco-Prussian War. After drafting several versions of this work, which he called *Le Chant du départ* (Farewell Song), he stuffed it in a drawer, dissatisfied.

Huysmans' attempts at finding his path as a writer were not especially successful, until one evening in 1875, when at a Wednesday night gathering in his apartment:

> He began to tell Bobin, Ludovic du Seigneur and Céard about his romantic misadventures while he was a student living on his own, apart from his family. He told about a passion he had felt for a woman who was an actress on the stage of the Bobino, and about the dull routine and boredom that eventually set in. In ironic and incisive details both funny and grim, he described the places and individuals.[11]

His friends, impressed by the verve and stark realism of his account, urged him to write a novel based on his experiences. They managed, after some initial reluctance on his part, to persuade him that he was meant for greater things than writing short essays about art. Huysmans agreed to attempt writing fiction based on his experiences.

Soon after this discussion, he revised and expanded the three-year-old manuscript about his war experiences into a long short story, changing its title from *Le Chant du départ* to 'Sac au dos'. This work, while it reads like fiction, is one of the most autobiographical of Huysmans' writings according to Huysmans himself. Soon after completing 'Sac au dos', he began work on a novel about a young man who has a love affair with an actress at the Bobino. While some aspects of the novel are probably autobiographical, Huysmans extended and embellished the plot, inventing secondary characters and focusing on the female protagonist. The novel, entitled *Marthe, histoire d'une fille* (Marthe, the Story of a Whore), developed into the account of a working-class woman who becomes a prostitute after more respectable professions fail to provide her with a decent livelihood. Because Huysmans had often visited brothels with his friends from the Ministry, the atmosphere, clients and prostitutes were familiar subject-matter. Indeed, he seems to have been fascinated by the garish decor, theatrical costumes and uninhibited behaviour he had observed. Since he had decided that at the novel's beginning his heroine would be an employee in an artificial pearl factory, he and Ludo visited such a factory; and because he had decided that a key character, Ginginet, would end up as a cadaver on a hospital morgue table, he asked his friend Céard, a former medical student, to arrange for him to observe an autopsy. It took some courage to approach the topic of prostitution in a novel. Although Balzac had explored the subject of the courtesan, Huysmans was arguably the first French writer to make a common prostitute the heroine of a novel. He knew that this subject was likely to arouse the hostilities of the censors. Other writers who had dared to discuss prostitution had been fined or even sent to prison. But Huysmans was determined to get his novel published as soon as possible. Although the prospect of being hauled before a tribunal cannot have been appealing, he sensed that a degree of notoriety would not be such a bad thing for a young writer just starting out. Furthermore, he liked the idea of scandalizing the bourgeois reading public.

Huysmans' novel, while based on careful research in the manner of Zola, could scarcely be called naturalistic. Much of the work depicts Marthe's distorted view of reality and her tendency to seek escape into altered states of consciousness. At times, she seems less a simple working-class girl than a poetic dreamer, for she gazes longingly at pictures by Hogarth and Jordaens of Bacchanalian revellers in faraway places, and is enchanted by the theatre because she can discard her own identity and become a seductive goddess. She is both entranced and repelled by life in the brothel; it appeals to her because here too she can play a role and change her identity. Near the end of the novel, Marthe slips into an alcohol-induced hallucination in which she sees herself entering the brothel for the first time, years earlier. She feels a powerful urge to return there, for in her mind it is a safe refuge, a world apart, where she can forget her life by taking on another identity:

> This was the attraction of the abyss over which one is leaning, that of a life lived at white heat, with its somersaults and pirouettes, the glasses emptied while lying on one's back . . . It was a deliberate abdication of day-to-day struggles. The brothel removed the difficulties of existence.[12]

Thus even in his first novel the main character shows a tendency to withdraw from the everyday world into the realm of artifice, as represented by the theatre and the brothel. Still, Huysmans takes pains to represent Marthe's moral and physical deterioration in a detailed, realistic fashion. Her loss of virtue is motivated by economics: she gives herself to a wealthy old man because she is hungry and has lost her job. After a failed attempt to become an actress, she enters a brothel and ends up in the gutter. While on the surface the novel seems a classic naturalist case study, the emphasis on dreams and hallucinations is already a sign of the path Huysmans would eventually take away from naturalism.

As Huysmans was completing *Marthe*, his mother died. Suddenly, he found himself responsible for his two young half-sisters, Juliette and Blanche, aged eleven and thirteen – and for the bookbindery that his mother had run. It is a testimony to his efficiency and determination that he was able to cope quickly with this emergency. In short order, he requested and was granted a leave from the Ministry of the Interior, took charge of the business's accounting books, turned over the day-to-day management of the bindery to a capable woman who was already working there and resumed work on his novel. It must be assumed that family members – likely his uncle Jules Badin and his wife, who lived nearby – took over much of the responsibility for the two girls. The two families had always been close, and it is known that Huysmans himself had spent a great deal of time at his uncle's house in his youth. A few months after his mother's death, he finished *Marthe*.

He had little time to celebrate the completion of his novel; in August 1876, he learned to his surprise that Edmond de Goncourt was putting the finishing touches to a novel that was also about a prostitute, entitled *La Fille Élisa* (Elisa the Prostitute). Worse still, the novel was set to be published very soon – in November 1876. Worried that Goncourt might steal his chance at notoriety and be the first to publish a novel featuring a prostitute as the main character, Huysmans decided to do whatever was necessary to publish *Marthe* first. Given the strict censorship laws in France and the reluctance of French publishers to accept a book on such a risky subject, he decided to go to Belgium, where censorship laws were much more liberal. In August 1876, still on leave from his job at the Ministry, he travelled to Brussels and sought out a Belgian writer named Camille Lemonnier, who was also the editor of a small journal called *L'Art universel* and had published some short pieces by Huysmans.

Lemonnier proved to be extremely helpful. He recommended a publisher, Jean Gay, who, being something of a specialist in books on erotic topics, immediately offered Huysmans a contract for the

Jean-Louis Forain, *J.-K. Huysmans*, 1878, pastel.

book, though at the author's expense. Huysmans accepted. He and Lemonnier spent much time together while Huysmans was in Brussels; besides showing Huysmans around the museums, taverns and brothels of the city, Lemonnier introduced him to a number of Belgian writers and artists. It was through Lemonnier that Huysmans met the poet Théodore Hannon and the graphic artist Félicien Rops, both of whom were to become his close friends.

Having arranged and paid for the speedy publication of *Marthe*, Huysmans went on to the Netherlands, where he visited his uncle Constant in Tilburg. Uncle Constant had a splendid collection of graphic art and he encouraged Huysmans to expect to inherit it. Upon returning to Brussels, Huysmans found that his book was already in print and in the bookstores. He attempted to bring four hundred copies of *Marthe* back to France, but most of the books were confiscated at the border by French customs. He had hoped that the novel's plain, inoffensive cover – and a moralistic disclaimer on the title page – would convince the French customs agents to let him bring the books into France, but the title *Marthe, histoire d'une fille* was enough to cause them to be seized. This resulted in his being sent a stern letter from the Ministry of the Interior, his employer, but there were no further repercussions. Once back home in Paris, Huysmans took the step of sending a copy of *Marthe* to Edmond de Goncourt, attaching a flattering note and describing (doubtless in order to get sympathy from the older, more famous writer) the ordeal with French customs. Goncourt wrote a gracious reply, praising the book, but offering some polite criticism as well. But, most of all, Huysmans was eager to give a copy to his new idol: Émile Zola, whose writings he had discovered a year earlier, and whom he considered to be as great or greater than Goncourt and Flaubert. Huysmans had used the meagre royalties he had received from *Le Drageoir aux épices* to buy all of Zola's early novels. When Zola's monumental *L'Assommoir* (The Dram Shop) appeared in serial form in *Le Bien public* in April 1876, Huysmans and his friends – except for Bobin, who disliked Zola's emphasis on determinism – became convinced that Zola was the writer who would blaze a new trail for the French novel. In April 1876 Céard had boldly called on Zola at his home and declared his admiration. The great man invited Céard to return and bring along his friends. Huysmans and Céard decided to visit him and Huysmans brought a copy of *Marthe*. Zola warmly welcomed Huysmans and Céard into his circle of young followers, and praised their writing as daring and contemporary – like his own. They had become members of the Médan group.

2

Under the Influence of Zola
and Naturalism

After meeting Zola and joining with other members of the
Médan group, including Guy de Maupassant and Léon Hennique,
Huysmans became a crusader for naturalism. This literary
movement, headed by Zola, advocated a kind of extreme realism
inspired by scientific advances. It portrayed human beings as
little more than the product of heredity, environment and animal
instincts. Huysmans believed that Zola had discovered a fresh,
true-to-life approach to the novel. He determined to write a series of
militant articles in defence of Zola's latest novel, *L'Assommoir*, which
had been publicly attacked amid accusations that the book and its
author were immoral. Huysmans' articles, grouped under the title
'Émile Zola et *L'Assommoir*', amounted to a naturalist manifesto
calling for an end to the sentimental novels of the romantic era and
their idealized portraits of ordinary men and women:

> We are men who believe that a writer, like a painter, should be
> of his own time; we are artists who are athirst with modernity
> . . . We go into the street, the living, teeming street, into hotel
> bedrooms as well as into fine mansions; into dark corners as well
> as into well-lit highways. We do not, like the romantics, want to
> create puppets more beautiful than nature, toned up every few
> pages, blurred and exalted by an optical illusion. We want to let
> creatures of flesh and blood stand on their own feet.[1]

Huysmans' fierce loyalty to Zola, whose daring new way of writing
he found enormously inspiring, made him eager to further the

cause by writing his own naturalist novel set in modern-day Paris depicting downtrodden workers living in its dreary industrial neighbourhoods. Casting about for an appropriate setting, he chose his mother's bookbindery, which was staffed entirely by women. After her death in 1876, he had been obliged to take over the direction of the business until a manager could be found and had become intrigued by the female workers. What better way, he thought, to portray modernity than by depicting their lives? This was a group that had previously been neglected or greatly romanticized by earlier authors. Following Zola's documentary method, he carefully studied the women as they toiled in the bindery, noting their dress, gestures and manner of speaking. Into this gritty setting, he introduced two main characters, Désirée and Céline Vatard, sisters struggling to eke out a living from their meagre wages. As he told Théo Hannon, he was determined to paint as true a picture of them as possible, trapped within the barriers imposed by social class and environment. At this point, Huysmans was both attracted to the common folk who worked in Paris's shops and factories, and repelled by them. He envied their freedom from bourgeois prudery and complacency and their ability to enjoy life's simple pleasures; but he was often disgusted by their ignorance and propensity for drinking and carousing. *Les Sœurs Vatard* (The Vatard Sisters), as he called the novel, reveals this ambivalence. As a way of rejecting his own bourgeois upbringing, he had begun haunting the dance halls, cafes and street fairs of the Latin Quarter, observing the rowdy men and women who gathered there to let off steam and drink cheap wine.

The novel has little plot and minimal character development but contains a number of memorable descriptions of the sisters' daily activities and dreary family life. At first, it seems a bit like an old-fashioned morality play, for the sisters are exact opposites: Céline is hot-blooded, lusty and irresponsible, while Désirée is prudent and virtuous, determined to save her virginity for marriage. When both girls meet men who court them, the reader wonders if Désirée will be rewarded for her goodness by finding happiness, and if Céline will be punished for her feckless behaviour. At first this does indeed seem to be the case: Céline's lover abuses her and they argue, while well-behaved Désirée is treated respectfully by her suitor and seems about to marry him. She even has hopes for the future. Her greatest wish is to marry a decent man and retreat to her own small, comfortable room, where she can at last

> realise her dream: to have a bedroom with floral wallpaper, a bed and a table of walnut wood, white curtains on the windows, a pincushion made of shells, a cup on the dresser with her initials in gilt, and, hanging on the wall, a nice picture of a little cupid knocking on a door. She even daydreamed about this engraving, which she'd seen in a bric-à-brac shop, and she imagined how comfortable and cheerful the room would be with this picture leaning against the mantelpiece . . . She'd never wanted anything more than this.[2]

In Désirée's dream of an ideal refuge we see the first example of a theme that can be found in most of Huysmans' novels after *Les Sœurs Vatard*.[3] At the end of the novel, the reader's expectations of a moralizing conclusion prove incorrect, and Huysmans unveils a surprise: both foolish Céline and her well-behaved sister end up alone and unhappy. Céline abandons her lover after they quarrel, while Désirée and her beau simply lose interest in each other. The sisters' failure to find love seems primarily due to the poverty and ignorance in which they live.

Les Sœurs Vatard is open to more than one interpretation. While some modern critics have noted that the novel expresses Huysmans' misogyny (neither Céline nor Désirée is particularly sensitive or intelligent), the same is true of most of the male characters. All are distressingly unaware of their plight as workers and are unable to think of much other than getting through each day. It should also be noted that the narrator, who frequently makes negative remarks about women, is not necessarily Huysmans himself, but more plausibly a working-class male observer, given his vocabulary and attitudes. The contrasting personalities of Céline and Désirée exemplify a dual view of women as either harlots or near saints that Huysmans was to develop further in later novels, such as *En route*.

Les Sœurs Vatard's strength is in its descriptions, often reminiscent of Impressionist paintings. Portrayals of Paris's teeming street life abound, bringing to life the colourful working-class neighbourhoods that Huysmans loved to explore:

> The street was crowded that evening. Cries of delight issued from the open windows of dance halls and from half-opened doors of bars. Groups of people were clustered on the pavement, bands of children were swarming around playing hide-and-seek and were threatened with a slap whenever they grabbed the jackets of men passing by. Near Jamin's café-concert hall . . . the crowd grew even thicker. At the door of this dance hall stood a uniformed doorman trying to look tough, and lads in baggy peaked caps and ruched shirts, with butterfly collars and no ties, took drags on their cigarettes, joking with girls trussed up from head to toe in long mackintoshes.[4]

In its depiction of late nineteenth-century Parisian popular culture, the novel is both intriguing and informative. Despite his rather mundane subject-matter, Huysmans strove to create new and surprising effects of style, which he called *feux d'artifice* (fireworks). He told Hannon that he was especially proud of a long description of a street fair, with its wine tents, gingerbread stands, strong men and fat ladies. Buskers' calls, taunts from the crowd, drinking songs and snippets of working-class chit-chat are all evoked with a deft hand, as in this passage describing the 'femmes colosse[s]' or fat ladies:

> Tubs of lard, sculpted into the shape of women, abounded at this fair. They were from every region and every taste: 'The Venus of Luchon', 'The Belle of Brabant', 'The Giantess of Auvergne'; disreputable-looking men armed with drumsticks punctuated their sales patter with drum rolls, pointing to signs that all

looked the same. Indeed, against a field of green and red, all of them displayed gigantic bellies with breasts like dumb-bells and legs like towers, and all these monstrous women splayed the immense hams of their thighs on red cushions.[5]

Once Huysmans had completed *Les Sœurs Vatard*, he submitted the manuscript to Charpentier, who had published several of Zola's novels. The master of Médan pressed Charpentier to accept his young friend's novel, but the editor hesitated, for Huysmans was not well known and it was not clear that this unorthodox book would sell well. During the many months he waited for a decision, Huysmans suffered frequent attacks of anxiety. To alleviate the stress, he plunged into a whirlwind of parties and dinners hosted by eminent literary figures, but he found these events boring, full of eager young writers seeking to get ahead by courting those who were successful. Fortunately he had another diversion that was more pleasant: Anna Meunier, a young seamstress with whom he had had a liaison some years earlier, came back into his life. She now had two young daughters, Antonine and Blanche, and was working in a store in the Latin Quarter. They resumed their relationship, spending evenings together, going on outings and discussing Huysmans' writing projects. In letters to Hannon from this period, Huysmans referred jocularly to the energetic lovemaking that he and Anna engaged in, remarking that there were days when the two did not leave his apartment, preferring to spend the day in bed together:

> I'm plugging away, but woe is me! I'm under the spell of a woman – poor me! A charming young shop girl has pulled me back into her nets. In my flat on the rue de Sèvres I'm singing libidinous love songs. My pure, chaste bedroom smells of woman! I had so firmly promised myself never again to have a mistress! Ah, poor me! Well – at least I'll have some pretty things to write about, one of these days! It will give me a few good pages.[6]

When at last Huysmans learned in mid-1878 that Charpentier had accepted *Les Sœurs Vatard* and the manuscript was at the printer's, he was overjoyed. He was also delighted when the novel's coarse vocabulary and cynical treatment of sexuality shocked readers. The furore surrounding his novel helped to sell it, and his new-found notoriety meant he was now a known figure in literary circles, albeit a disreputable one. Zola was happy to see a naturalist work by one of his disciples attracting attention; he published a glowing review of *Les Sœurs Vatard* that boosted sales of the book even further. Two other mentors, Flaubert and Goncourt, were complimentary but somewhat less enthusiastic. Both acknowledged that the novel was skilfully written and that Huysmans was a promising young writer. However, Flaubert chided him for pontificating about naturalism in the novel, while Goncourt urged him to stop writing about poor, uninteresting characters and instead to choose more refined subject-matter, remarking that *L'Assommoir* and *Les Sœurs Vatard* 'have at this point exhausted what I'll call "literary rabble". I exhort you to choose as milieu for your next novel a different sphere, a higher sphere' ('ont à l'heure qu'il est épuisé ce que j'appellerai *la canaille littéraire*, et je vous engage à choisir pour milieu de votre prochain livre, une sphère autre, une sphère supérieure').[7] This advice ran counter to Zola's theories, causing Huysmans to do some serious thinking about his own goals as a writer.

Once *Les Sœurs Vatard* was published, Huysmans, elated by the novel's successful sales, dived into several new projects. Among them was a series of articles in the journal *Le Voltaire* about the paintings on display at the Paris Salon of 1879. His articles attacked some of the most highly regarded artists of the day, mocking their conventional techniques and subject-matter, while extolling the Impressionists for their innovative rendering of modern life. The editorial staff of *Le Voltaire* were horrified when they read his sarcastic comments. A number of artists who had been maligned immediately demanded that *Le Voltaire* cease publishing Huysmans' reviews. Had Zola not fiercely defended him, the magazine might well have decided not to accept more of his work.

Feeling full of rebellious energy, Huysmans began work on a new novel, taking Goncourt's advice to focus on characters living in a 'different sphere', who were more complex and refined than those of *Les Sœurs Vatard*. This time he chose as protagonist a middle-class writer, André Jayant, a man unsure of his goals in life. André's best friend, Cyprien Tibaille, is an avant-garde painter who scorns bourgeois values and aims to create a more modern form of art. Both characters have some traits in common with Huysmans. In contrast with the uneventful plot of *Les Sœurs Vatard*, *En ménage* (Living Together) offers a degree of suspense that holds the reader's interest. At the beginning of the novel André surprises his wife in bed with another man and, realizing that his marriage is a failure, he decides to leave her and resume his former life as a bachelor. The book traces his attempts to find a suitable female companion who will see to his needs without making many demands. He has a relationship with a high-class prostitute that proves unsatisfactory, then with Jeanne, a former girlfriend. But ultimately he decides these women are no better than his wife, and so he returns to her. His wife seems equally resigned to a lukewarm marriage; when they reunite, neither has much hope that they will be happy together:

> They went out into the street, meditative, dumb, obsessed by the same preoccupations, worried and contented at the same time, thinking of the whole messed-up life together which they were going to start up again, afraid that in spite of the experience they had acquired, they might ruin it for ever.[8]

There is considerably more character development in this novel than in *Les Sœurs Vatard*: André is portrayed as a meek, mild man who had an unhappy childhood and has become an adult who, though well read and intelligent, has no ambition. He wants little more from marriage than sex and a clean house. His wife, who was spoiled by her wealthy father, longs for a romantic, exciting husband, which clearly André is not. The two are mismatched and self-centred, unable to build a caring relationship. The novel's plot offers Huysmans ample opportunity to make cynical remarks about marriage, an institution he assiduously avoided. *En ménage* includes a number of interior monologues in which André attempts to find solutions to his personal difficulties. In addition to his marital woes, he finds he is unable to write; in fact, it is not clear that he has ever been able to produce much:

> He sat in front of his desk, saw the scene he wanted to describe, grasped his pen and stayed motionless like those people who have waited for dinner a long time and are unable to swallow a morsel as soon as they are sitting at table.
>
> He tore his paper in a rage. He would not have needed much to think himself mad. He feared his intelligence had been warped. He was desolate, thinking he would be for ever impotent, then he reacted, remembered a few good pages he had previously written, to strengthen his courage.[9]

This novel is Huysmans' first to feature a writer, albeit a failed one, as protagonist. It is also partly autobiographical, especially the episode in which André reconnects with his former mistress, Jeanne. A signed copy of *En ménage* that he gave to Anna Meunier bears the inscription 'À Jeanne – Anna Meunier'. This leaves little doubt that Anna served as a model for Jeanne and suggests that the affair between André and Jeanne is partly based on Huysmans' often rocky relationship with Anna. When *En ménage* was published, the critical reaction was generally unfavourable. However, the painters Cézanne and Pissarro were delighted by it, as was Zola.

After *En ménage* was published in 1881, Huysmans felt exhausted and ill. He told his friends he was suffering from overwrought nerves and neuralgia. Acting on the advice of his doctor, he decided to rent a house in the village of Fontenay-aux-Roses, just outside Paris, in order to recuperate. This was not a holiday; he continued to report for work at the Ministry of the Interior, taking the train into Paris each morning. Despite his health problems, he was working hard on a novel he had started and set aside some years earlier. This novel, *La Faim* (Hunger), was supposed to be an ambitious account of life in Paris during the terrible Prussian siege of Paris in 1870–71. Anna had furnished a great deal of information for it, and he intended to make a character resembling her the protagonist.[10] But he was unable to find inspiration and eventually set aside the project, turning to a different idea: a novel that would further develop some of the themes of *En ménage*. He had been reading Schopenhauer's *Aphorisms* and was increasingly convinced that few, if any, human beings are able to find happiness, and that most merely muddle through life with dreary stoicism. While *En ménage* had portrayed a bourgeois protagonist who is financially secure and does not need to work for a living, Huysmans now decided to write about an underpaid employee whose life cycles ever downward in a series of small but devastating disappointments. He called it *À vau-l'eau* (Drifting). This Everyman, M. Folantin, is a low-level government clerk who toils at a meaningless job and tries timidly to find a modicum of happiness. His attempts to alleviate his loneliness by starting a relationship with a woman fail miserably; a friendly woman he meets in a shop turns out to be a floozy who leaves him with a venereal disease. After several more futile attempts to find female companionship, he decides to pursue a smaller goal: to find a restaurant where he can enjoy a decent meal. This attempt also proves unsuccessful, for everywhere he goes the meals he can afford are disgusting and inedible. (Huysmans' friends immediately recognized this obsession as a hallmark of Huysmans himself.) The novel ends on a more deeply pessimistic note than *En ménage*, for M. Folantin is still alone, unable to afford a comfortable room or even a proper meal, and tormented by attacks of indigestion caused by the unappetizing food he has been eating. He has lost all hope; religion seems only fit for the witless, and so he cannot turn to it for consolation. M. Folantin has been compared to other literary prototypes of alienation such as Sartre's Roquentin and Camus' Meursault, but he differs from them in that he seems to have deep-seated spiritual longings, though he rejects them as illogical, absurd:

> What better occupation than prayer? What better avocation than confession? What better release than the practice of religion? . . .
>
> Yes, but why are the consolations of religion only fit for simpletons? Why did the Church want to elevate the most absurd beliefs into dogmatic truths? There's no way I can accept either the virginity of an expectant mother, or the divinity of a comestible prepared by a breadmaker, and besides, the intolerance of the clergy revolted him. And yet mysticism alone could heal the wound that torments me. All the same, it would be wrong to point out to the faithful the futility of their devotions, because if they can accept all the vexations, all the afflictions of their present life as a passing trial they are happy indeed.[11]

Besides writing fiction and art criticism, Huysmans had become involved in another kind of project. In 1880 he joined Zola and several other members of the naturalist group in a bold new venture: a literary magazine, to be called *La Comédie humaine* (The Human Comedy). The mission of *La Comédie humaine* was to promote the naturalist cause by providing an outlet for talented writers who, like Zola and his followers, wanted to embrace modernity and reject romanticism. Excited by this project, and no doubt thinking it would advance his own career, Huysmans agreed to become editor in chief and immediately began soliciting submissions from writers whom he admired, and who were sympathetic to the tenets of naturalism. Among those he contacted were his close friend the Belgian poet Théo Hannon and Edmond de Goncourt, who was already an established author with a unique style of his own. Problems developed as the financial support for the magazine fell through and the publisher backed away. The last straw came when Zola proposed a drastic change in the nature of the magazine, urging that instead of a longer publication open to a wide variety of writers, *La Comédie humaine* should be a short pamphlet of only a few pages per issue. More distressingly, Zola also insisted on limiting contributors to his own circle of followers – in other words, to members of the Médan group. This would have excluded Goncourt and Hannon. Huysmans hotly disagreed, writing to Hannon about his reaction to Zola's proposal:

> I refused and pointed out that a magazine closed in such a way went against all my ideas. That it would be totally monotonous and lead to literary sterility with no financial gain to the few people who would write for it. I added that I had the issue ready and that if it was not accepted I would resign, if my friends were rejected.
>
> A disagreement followed. Zola persisted in his idea of founding a short journal. With that, I resigned as editor in chief. So I'm no longer part of *La Comédie humaine*.[12]

La Comédie humaine never appeared in print, and the entire venture failed. Huysmans had wasted considerable time without financial compensation, and he was worried that the writers he had invited to publish their work in the magazine would blame him. This was one of the first real disagreements between Huysmans and Zola, and it likely kindled a latent resentment in him that slowly grew over time. Though on the surface their relationship continued to be cordial, he was beginning to feel that Zola was too authoritarian and egotistical, and that if he was to develop his own individual style of writing, he needed to assert his independence.

As he completed *À vau-l'eau*, he was also beginning to question Zola's theories, finding that he had more in common with Edmond de Goncourt, whose writing he had admired long before discovering Zola's works. The failure of *La Comédie humaine* and the loss of his position as editor in chief still weighed upon him. During this time, he read and was profoundly impressed by Goncourt's *La Maison d'un artiste* (An Artist's House), a book that describes in exquisite detail the author's art-filled home in Paris. That a man's love for his house could be the subject of a book was a revelation. Huysmans had never been fond of concocting complex plots, and Goncourt's skilful descriptions of the paintings, books and *objets d'art* in his home were especially intriguing to him; he was something of a collector himself. Concerning *La Maison d'un artiste*, he wrote to Goncourt: 'What is adorable and in every way exquisite . . . is the profound love for the house and the beautiful things that inhabit it. That's present on every page. There's a delicious intimacy here that moves me and gives me a gentle, nervous shiver when I read certain pages.'[13] He also told Goncourt that his own ambition to be a writer had first been inspired by reading the older author's works, declaring:

> If I've had an ambition to be a writer, it is to your books that I owe it. It was your novels that were the first to grip me, and it is to them that I always return in hours of sadness, for they alone exude the intimate melancholy of existence.[14]

As Huysmans was mulling over ideas for a new novel, the notion of making a uniquely decorated house central to the plot appealed to him. The frisson he had felt reading Goncourt's *Maison d'un artiste* recurred when he read the older writer's newest novel, *La Faustin*, in which a celebrated actress at the pinnacle of her career is overcome by grief after a failed love affair. Though Huysmans was no romantic – nor was Goncourt – the novel left an unsettling impression on him; as he told Goncourt, he was struck by the 'psychological dissection, detailing sensations and reveries that until now had been inexpressible' ('une dissection psychologique, détaillant des sensations, des songeries jusqu'à ce jour inexprimées').[15] The main character's emotional torments seem to have propelled him into a state of nervous ecstasy, inspiring him to try new approaches in his own writing.

Other influences on Huysmans at this time were his new-found interests in the effects of art and literature on the nervous system, and in 'expressing the inexpressible'. They were about to manifest themselves in a groundbreaking novel that would stun

Paris's literary world. His discovery of several unconventional artists helped spark a desire to incorporate works of art into his own writing. While the Impressionists continued to appeal to him with their depictions of the real world in fleeting, ever-changing glimpses, he had become entranced by painters whose images seemed inspired by dreams and fantasy. The art of Odilon Redon and Gustave Moreau made him long for realms far beyond reality. By the autumn of 1882 he was working hard on a new book that he knew would astound all who read it, for not only was it entirely different from anything he had written before but it was different from anything that anyone else had written as well. In October 1882 he wrote to his colleague Stéphane Mallarmé, calling the novel 'quite a singular story', and describing its protagonist as a decadent aristocrat who, disgusted with the world's materialism, takes refuge in solitude and fantasy:

> Out of disgust with American lifestyle, contempt for the aristocracy of wealth, the last representative of an illustrious family takes refuge in definitive solitude.
>
> He is cultured, of the most refined delicacy. In his comfortable retreat, he seeks to replace monotonous, humdrum nature with artifice; he enjoys the writers of the exquisite and penetrating period of Roman decadence. I am using the word decadence so as to be intelligible; he even flings himself into the Latin of the Church, into the barbaric and delicious poems of Orientius, Veranius of Gévaudan, Baudonivia, etc., etc. In French he is mad about Poe, Baudelaire, the second part of *La Faustin*. You can see what it is going to be like.[16]

In the same letter Huysmans asked Mallarmé to send him copies of several now-famous poems, so that he could include commentary on them in the novel. His profound admiration for Mallarmé, whom he had recently met, is an indicator of Huysmans' growing fondness for writing that was original and innovative, belonging to no school or movement.

The new book, initially entitled *Seul* (Alone), was only just beginning to take shape at this point, Huysmans knew he was writing something unusual, but he could never have imagined that this novel, which he jokingly described to friends as 'very strange', would stun the Parisian literary world and influence writers far beyond France's borders. He decided to call it *À rebours* (Against Nature).

3

À rebours and Beyond

Huysmans had been sure that his strange book would be an utter
failure, quickly forgotten by the few who had bothered to read it.
But when *À rebours* was published by Charpentier in May 1884
the opposite proved to be true. His novel shocked and intrigued
its readers. Instead of presenting a number of realistically drawn
characters, like most fiction at the time, it focused on a single, solitary
protagonist: Des Esseintes, a profoundly neurotic nobleman who
isolates himself in a country mansion decorated with hallucinatory
paintings. Instead of a clearly defined plot, the novel is virtually
plotless: the only action that takes place is in the protagonist's head.
Rather than advancing the narrative, each successive chapter is
devoted to an aspect of Des Esseintes' house and its bizarre decor:
exotic flowers that appear diseased, arcane books, a collection of
perfumes with which he paints imaginary pictures in the air, and
a tortoise whose shell is encrusted with rare jewels. Des Esseintes
retreats to this place in order to escape the real world, which he finds
vulgar and depressing. Because he does not wish to leave the house,
he decorates it in ways that enable him to travel in his imagination.
One room simulates a ship's cabin, encircled by aquariums full of
mechanical fish, with windows like portholes: 'Travel, indeed, struck
him as being a waste of time, since he believed that the imagination
could provide a more-than-adequate substitute for the vulgar reality
of actual experience.'[1]

Another room is designed to resemble a monk's cell, though
only the richest, most sensually pleasing materials have been used
to decorate it. Des Esseintes wants to thumb his nose at religion by

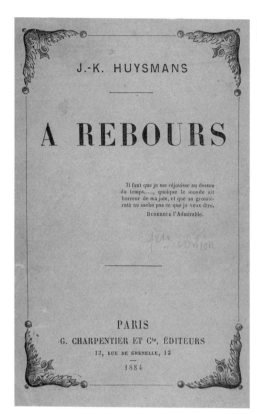

Title page to *À rebours* (1884).

imagining unspeakable acts there. In the private universe he has created, he indulges in exotic fantasies, exercising mind control in order to obliterate the annoyances of real life: 'The main thing is to know how to set about it, to be able to concentrate your attention on a single detail, to forget yourself sufficiently to bring about the desired hallucination and so substitute the vision of a reality for the reality itself.'[2]

Above all, Des Esseintes despises nature, which he considers to be crude and boring; instead, he prefers artifice: 'Nature, he used to say, has had her day; she has finally and utterly exhausted the patience of sensitive observances by the revolting uniformity of her landscapes and skyscapes.'[3]

Odilon Redon's frontispiece for *À rebours*, portraying Des Esseintes.

But Des Esseintes misjudges his ability to control the little world he has created. In particular, Gustave Moreau's two depictions of Salome, the biblical femme fatale who caused the death of John the Baptist, prove to have an unsettling effect. In Moreau's watercolour *L'Apparition* (The Apparition), Salome, seductively clad, is transfixed by a vision of John the Baptist's severed head. She has stopped her lascivious dance and is frozen in fear. For Des Esseintes, she is at once alluring and dangerous. The description is highly erotic:

> She is almost naked; in the heat of the dance her veils have fallen away and her brocade robes slipped to the floor, so that now she is clad only in wrought metals and translucent gems. A gorgerin grips her waist like a corselet, and like an outsize clasp a wondrous jewel sparkles and flashes in the cleft between her breasts; lower down, a girdle encircles her hips, hiding the upper part of her thighs, against which dangles a gigantic pendant glistening with rubies and emeralds . . .
>
> Here she was a true harlot, obedient to her passionate and cruel female temperament; here she came to life, more refined yet more savage, more hateful yet more exquisite than before; here she roused the sleeping senses of the male more powerfully, subjugated his will more surely with her charms – the charms of a great venereal flower, grown in a bed of sacrilege, reared in a hot-house of impiety.[4]

Unexpectedly, Moreau's paintings of Salome trigger previously repressed phobias and compulsions concerning women and sex, and Des Esseintes has a terrifying nightmare in which he is pursued by the androgenous figure of syphilis. The dream seems partly inspired by the exotic flowering plants he has collected, especially a Nidularium with petals like sword blades that becomes a frightening woman in his dream.

After the nightmare, Des Esseintes' ideal refuge begins to fall apart and he is assailed by a variety of maladies. He loses his appetite, is unable to sleep and is no longer able to live in his

Gustave Moreau, *The Apparition*, 1876, watercolour.

6ᵉ volume.　　　　　N° 263. — 10 c.　　　　Un an : 6 fr.

LES HOMMES D'AUJOURD'HUI

DESSIN DE COLL-TOC

Bureaux : Librairie Vanier, 19, quai Saint-Michel, à Paris

J. K. HUYSMANS

Les Hommes d'aujourd'hui magazine cover, 1885.

own private dream world. Finally, he heeds his doctors' advice and reluctantly returns to Paris, the very place he had wanted to escape.

Although it is often assumed that Huysmans wrote *À rebours* as an act of rebellion against Zola and naturalism, this was likely not the case, though he did turn away from Zola a few years later. The notion that Huysmans' most famous and notorious novel was intended to demolish naturalism, or at least to undermine it, came in part from the author himself in his preface to *À rebours*, written in 1903, almost twenty years after the novel had first appeared. By then he was deeply immersed in conservative Catholicism and had rejected Zola's stark realism in favour of a more introspective style and deeply religious subject-matter. In his preface Huysmans claims that *À rebours* was inspired by a 'need to open up the windows, to flee from a milieu where I was suffocating'.[5] Here Huysmans also states that Zola was unable to understand this desire for a new approach to the novel. Despite Huysmans' implication that he was fed up with Zola and naturalism, it is important to realize that when he wrote *À rebours* he still considered himself a naturalist, and he and Zola were still friends. It seems probable that the older Huysmans who wrote the preface allowed his negative feelings about naturalism to distort the truth. It is more likely that *À rebours* was a kind of innovative experiment, an effort to renew his creative energies, with little or no ideological purpose. During the period when he was working on the novel, he told Zola and others about two naturalist works that he intended to finish: *La Faim*, the partly written novel inspired by Anna Meunier's experiences in Paris under the Prussian siege of 1870–71, and a nearly completed novel about murderers, thieves and prostitutes living in the unsavoury district of Paris known as Le Gros Caillou. Although he tried to continue working on both projects after completing *À rebours*, he eventually abandoned them. *À rebours* had changed him in ways he had not foreseen, and it changed the course of French literature as well, for the book was a bombshell. It did indeed break free from the limits of the novel and opened new horizons for a generation of younger writers. In addition, it addressed a number of key concerns and obsessions that were prevalent in the society of the time, including a desire to escape the dull realities of life, a new interest in neurosis and other psychological conditions, and hatred of the bourgeoisie, which was viewed by intellectuals as decadent.

After the publication of *À rebours*, Huysmans and Zola maintained a cordial relationship. As was his custom with his younger protégés, Zola wrote a detailed letter to Huysmans concerning the novel. Overall, it was favourable, though it also contained criticism. In conclusion Zola wrote: 'There is an outrageous artistry that delights me; such intensely original sensations are enough to put you in a superior category, all by yourself . . . This book will at least be a curiosity in your works, and you should be proud of having written it.'[6]

À rebours may at first have been a fanciful experiment, intended to be a way of renewing his creative energies, but it turned out to be difficult and exhausting to write. The novel had aggravated Huysmans' own 'personal neurosis', and he needed to distance himself. Despite encouraging comments from members of the Médan group, he had doubts about the book and wondered if it had been worth writing. The portrayal of Des Esseintes was seriously flawed, he felt. When *À rebours* was published in late May 1884, he told Zola: 'Basically, you see, it was a book not to write because it was much too difficult with this floating character such as I had conceived him.'[7]

While he was accustomed to negative reviews, he was upset by the ferocious attacks that the work provoked, telling Zola that *À rebours* had managed to infuriate all manner of disparate groups: Catholics and anticlericals, romantics and naturalists. 'I had this crazy book in my head, I released it and there's the end of it.'[8] Happily, a number of writers and critics whom Huysmans respected wrote favourable reviews of the novel. Léon Bloy, a renegade writer whom Huysmans had never met, published a glowing essay full of hyperbole about the novel, and as a result the two formed a close friendship. A flood of congratulatory letters from contemporary writers declaring the work a masterpiece

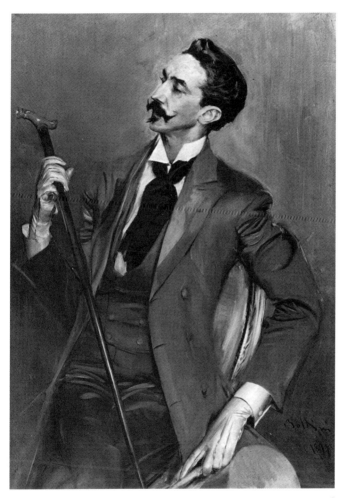

Giovanni Boldini, *Count Robert de Montesquiou*, 1897, oil on canvas. Montesquiou is said to have inspired Huysmans' Des Esseintes.

arrived in the months following the publication of *À rebours*. Among those who wrote were two valued friends, the Belgian writers Théo Hannon and Camille Lemonnier. Lemonnier praised the description of Des Esseintes' neurosis as especially well drawn: 'However hard I look, I don't think that any other modern book creates that strange sense of all the diabolical torments that your hero Des Esseintes suffers. It's a flaming red, neurotic hell.'[9]

Though he appreciated this praise and found it reassuring, overall Huysmans felt a strong urge to move on to new projects and to forget his 'toquade' (whim or caprice), which had left him drained and plagued by a variety of physical and psychological problems. He complained to Lemonnier: 'This volume literally killed me; I was afraid of a literary blow-up . . . I'll never write another book like that!'[10]

Where might he turn to find a new project? The next book would need to be very different – one that would soothe his tattered nerves and calm his neurosis; something less frenetic, more deliberate. Not long after completing *À rebours*, he quickly wrote a short naturalistic novella, *Un dilemme* (A Dilemma). This was not an experimental work like *À rebours*; it had a clear plot and featured a number of rather stereotypical characters. *Un dilemme* paints a repugnant picture of the bourgeoisie, telling the story of a poor, working-class woman who gives birth out of wedlock. When her bourgeois lover, the father of the baby, dies, his heartless family members refuse to help, leaving the mother and her child destitute. Huysmans declared that he had written this novella to express his profound hatred of the bourgeoisie. He does not seem to have been especially pleased with this work, and there are few comments about it in his correspondence.

It was a time of artistic uncertainty for him, as he worked on several very different pieces, including an essay on Gustave Moreau, whose paintings he had described at length in *À rebours*. He also tried to resume work on *La Faim*. But he told Zola that work on *La Faim* was not going well, lamenting that it was 'tormenting me greatly, on account of the very simplicity of the context. I am splashing about for the moment.'[11] Not long after this, he gave up on *La Faim* and set the manuscript aside. Another project he was working on was a long short story that he described as 'simple and calm', a sort of antidote to the frantic neurosis of *À rebours*. That long short story would gradually grow into a remarkable novel, *En rade* (Stranded).

He had discovered the perfect setting for his story: a rambling, semi-abandoned castle called the Château de Lourps, a place he had visited several times. It may seem odd that a die-hard urban dweller like Huysmans should decide to go on holiday to a ruined castle lost in the countryside; but buried deep down under his sardonic, citified exterior was a latent romantic, a poetic dreamer who embraced the idea of escaping to a forbidding castle that seemed straight out of a novel by Dumas or Chateaubriand. In 1881 he and Anna had visited the Château de Lourps while staying in the nearby village of Jutigny, not far from Provins, in north-central France. Anna's friend Virginie Bescherer, wife of the engraver Louis Bescherer, was from Jutigny and had told them about the village and the surrounding area. From the start, Huysmans must have been intrigued by the castle and the village,

Château de Lourps, Longueville.

for he went back there on holiday over the years between 1881 and 1886, sometimes alone, and sometimes with Anna. Not until 1885, however, did he actually stay at the castle, accompanied by Anna, her young daughter Antonine and Anna's sister Joséphine. He was delighted by Lourps. While he admitted it was 'une ruine', and that of its two hundred rooms only five or six were habitable, he enthusiastically described the pleasures of life there to his old friend Alexis Orsat:

> During the day, I daydream along the delicious woodland paths, I read on the lawn. I live in perfect serenity. In the evening, when we are by ourselves, bézigue helps pass the time, and besides, there is the bed.
> I'm on my honeymoon of solitude. I hope it will last.[12]

If Huysmans enjoyed his stay at Lourps, Anna Meunier was less enthusiastic. She found the nights there frightening, for the wind howled through the broken windows and owls flew hooting through the bedroom: 'On the other hand, Anna is feeling dead-tired just now. She isn't sleeping well, and at night she's terrified by the long dark corridors, the echo of our footsteps, and the shindy made by the birds when night falls.'[13]

A few years later, when Anna developed a mysterious neurological illness, Huysmans wondered if her frightening experience at Lourps had somehow caused her malady, and he blamed himself for taking her there, for she was emotionally fragile. At the time, however, Huysmans made light of Anna's fears and immersed himself in the castle's picturesque decay. His emerging romantic leanings, especially his love of nature, are clear in a letter he wrote to his friends Léon Bloy and Georges Landry, in which he describes Lourps and its overgrown gardens:

> I have taken over the defunct château de Lourps, a château of fine appearance, with a dovecote, former moat and two hundred bedrooms. The park, torn apart and bought up bit by bit by the peasants, is still delightful, returned to its natural state, with

Anna Meunier, Huysmans' long-time companion.

flowers growing haphazardly, full of delightful paths, through the woods for leisurely walks, a beautiful dream of sunlit verdure, an orgy of ivy eating into the blue pines, a debauchery of doves and swallows in the eaves of the château . . . which is abandoned, ruined, divided up, exquisite with its vaults of times gone by, its trellises, its door giving on to the church, which is invaded by lichen and inhabited by crows.[14]

If Huysmans was drawn to the poetic decrepitude of the castle and its delightfully neglected gardens, perhaps it was because he was feeling a melancholy kinship with the place; for despite the cheerful tone in his correspondence, he was exhausted, yearning for stability and peace of mind. His position at the Ministry bored and frustrated him; he was poorly paid and felt bullied by his supervisor. In addition, he was beset by serious financial worries concerning the bookbindery, which he and his half-sisters still owned. The temporary escape to the Château de Lourps suited his mood; and he found his health was improving. But he was also a realist about Lourps, warning his two friends that if they came to visit, they were apt to find the accommodation uncomfortable:

> As for the naturalist aspect, that is different. It is like being shipwrecked!!! One is further away from everything than if one were on an island distant from any continent. In order to get bread, one has to put a basket at the bottom of the immense and noble drive, decimated, alas, by devious felling . . .[15]

Besides relaxing, Huysmans was taking careful notes about the appearance of the castle at different hours of the day – sunset, afternoon, evening – and he was studying the architecture of both the castle and the adjoining church. *En rade* was now beginning to take shape in his mind, though at this point he still expected it to be a long short story. The following summer, in 1886, he returned to Lourps, where he began writing in earnest. By October the story was turning into a novel, and he told Zola: 'I'm working hard, immersed in writing a piece that I had intended to be a novella . . .

It has turned into a kind of novel! – so that now it will be a book all by itself.'[16] Huysmans worked quickly. In late 1886, before *En rade* was even finished, he decided to allow the early chapters to appear in serial form. It was published as a book in 1887 by Tresse & Stock.

There can be no question that *En rade* marks a decisive departure from Huysmans' previous novels. It is every bit as original and perplexing as *À rebours*, though in it Huysmans returns to a more traditional technique of portraying several carefully drawn characters rather than one solitary protagonist. It resembles *À rebours* in that a house (or in this case, a castle) is central to the novel. The crumbling Château de Lourps is not just the setting of *En rade*; it is in a sense the main character, for it appears, in different lighting and in different moods, on almost every page. The enigmatic structure looms over the human characters who live inside it. It influences their thoughts and emotions, particularly in the case of the troubled protagonist Jacques Marles. As he approaches the castle at the beginning of the novel, it appears sinister, even menacing, its windows reflecting the red sunset sky. From the start, there is a mysterious connection between Jacques and this crumbling edifice:

> The imposing fortissimo of the sunset had given way to the mournful silence of an ashen sky; here and there, however, the odd unconsumed ember glowed red among the smoke of the clouds and lit the château from behind, striking the haughty ridge of the roof, the lofty form of the chimney and the two towers . . . Illuminated like this, the château seemed like a burnt-out ruin in which a badly extinguished fire was still smouldering . . . The sight of this château that still seemed to be burning dully exacerbated his state of nervous agitation, which had been steadily growing since the morning.[17]

Jacques Marles has come to Lourps with his ailing wife Louise to get away from their financial and personal difficulties. Louise's aunt and uncle are caretakers of the château and have invited them to live there temporarily. While the château is often gloomy and brooding, it can also take on a joyous, welcoming appearance, depending on the effects of sun and shadows. These varying portraits of the same building seen in different kinds of light were probably inspired by the Impressionists, especially Monet's series of paintings of Rouen Cathedral. Certainly, the descriptions of the château and the difficulties of daily life there, along with often unflattering portraits of the local peasants, were inspired in part by Huysmans' own experiences while at Lourps. During the fictional couple's stay at Lourps, Louise begins to suffer from a strange, debilitating illness that partially paralyses her. It is likely that the passages describing her symptoms came from his observations of the illness that Anna Meunier was beginning to develop, and which eventually caused her death.[18]

It would be a mistake to assume that *En rade* is exactly modelled on Huysmans' own experiences, however; Jacques' perception of Lourps is far more grim than Huysmans'. Though, like Huysmans, Jacques is intrigued by Lourps, his mood is darker; he does not feel joy or love of nature as Huysmans did. Nor does the unpleasant picture of the peasants in *En rade* accurately reflect Huysmans' own more balanced feelings; he told Zola that he enjoyed spending time with them and found them picturesque and informative.

The novel's originality lies in its abrupt juxtaposition of real life and dreams. Mundane descriptions of daily life at the castle and the difficulties of making one room livable and obtaining provisions from the village alternate with long passages detailing Jacques' three otherworldly dreams. Along with these two versions of Jacques' stay at Lourps, there is the castle itself, with its decaying walls, broken windows and empty, dust-filled rooms. It seems to be both a part of reality, and an aspect of the world of dreams. Although it does not appear in Jacques' dreams, one senses that it somehow influences them – even triggers them. One dream, for example, occurs as Jacques stares at the design on the wallpaper in his bedroom.

In contrast to his bleak waking life, Jacques' three dreams are bright, bizarre and exotic. The first dream, reminiscent of Moreau's paintings of Salome in *À rebours*, is of a sultry, naked girl dancing in front of an elderly king. As he dreams, Jacques realizes this dream is an enactment of the biblical story of Esther. There is no explanation of the dream, though when he awakes he struggles to decipher its meaning. Two more strange dreams follow: one in which Jacques and Louise find themselves lost on the surface of the moon, and another about a beautiful woman whose eyes pop out. These dreams seem to have no bearing on Jacques' waking life, but they certainly reveal a rich trove of creativity within his unconscious. At this time, Huysmans was interested in the psychology of dreams and was reading widely on the topic, as well as recording his own dreams.[19]

The conclusion of *En rade* is not unlike the ending of *À rebours*. Just as in the latter novel, the protagonist's attempt to find a safe refuge fails – this time because Jacques and Louise realize they are being exploited by her aunt and uncle, on whom they depend in order to live in the château. Like *À rebours*, the novel ends as Jacques and Louise pack up their possessions and prepare to return to their unhappy life in Paris. The juxtaposition of dreams and reality in this novel inspired André Breton and the Surrealists, who considered *En rade* a masterpiece. Readers during Huysmans' day were less enthusiastic, but a few writers recognized its originality and admired Huysmans' bold new approach. Zola was not among those admirers; he was puzzled and felt that Huysmans should have clearly separated the real and dream worlds to make the novel less confusing. In fact, what is unique and subversive about *En rade*, as Brendan King points out, is that Huysmans

uses the conventions of Naturalism, both in his descriptions of the real world – as in his depiction of the crumbling château where the fabric of reality itself seems to be dissolving even as it is being described – and in his evocations of the dream world, where Naturalistic details are used to reify the purely imaginary and give it concrete substance.[20]

During the period of 1885–7, as Huysmans prepared and published *En rade*, several important events occurred in his personal life.

In late 1885, while he was at the Château de Lourps with Anna, her daughter and her sister, he received a letter from a young aspiring Dutch writer, Arij Prins. Prins was an admirer of Huysmans' novels and had written an essay about *En ménage*. He asked for more information about Huysmans and several other French authors for a series of articles he was preparing about contemporary French literature. Huysmans was flattered by Prins' interest in him and pleased to hear from a writer living in the Netherlands, a country that was part of his heritage. He responded warmly. Soon the two began a voluminous correspondence that has proved to be immensely useful to students and scholars. There were distressing events at this time as well, foremost of which was the death in March 1886 of a close friend, Robert Caze. Caze, a young poet and novelist, lost his life in a duel, leaving his ailing widow with a heavy burden of unpaid debts. In order to help Mme Caze, Huysmans and others collected a sum of money so that she could pay off her husband's debts and provide for her children. He told Prins:

> We're going to do whatever is necessary to help this poor woman out of her difficulties. We hope to obtain a scholarship for the little boy and we're going to try to find a safe place for the little girl. We're also going to provide for this unhappy woman as quickly as possible, so that she doesn't die of hunger.[21]

Huysmans also told Prins that this fatal duel had been 'for a nonsensical matter' ('pour une niaiserie').[22] Some months later his beloved cat, Barre-de-Rouille, died of a paralysing disease. The cat's death greatly upset Anna Meunier, who was suffering from intermittent paralysis. In *En rade* there is a description of a dying cat, written after Huysmans had witnessed Barre-de-Rouille's demise. In the novel Louise sees the cat's illness as a foreshadowing of her own death. Huysmans wrote: 'My wife is in tears . . . Anna adored him, calling him "her ginger baby" ('Ma femme[23] en larmes . . . Anna adorait ce qu'elle appelait son enfant rouge').[24] Not long after this, his friend Odilon Redon lost his infant son. Huysmans was deeply affected and did his best to console the heartbroken parents. In a melancholy letter to Prins at the end of 1886, he lamented: 'Mort de toutes parts' ('Death is everywhere').[25]

There were happy events as well. Early in 1887 Huysmans was promoted at the Ministry of the Interior to *sous-chef* (deputy chief clerk/assistant manager). This was an advancement he had sought and he was pleased by it. But he still hated the job, which he felt was too time-consuming (though he apparently had sufficient spare time to write most of his books during work hours). Concerning the promotion, he remarked: 'While I'm pleased to be promoted – I'll at least be able to have almost enough to eat – I'm also overwhelmed with work and aggravated by all the office infighting. It's impossible to do my own writing.'[26]

His immediate superior, whom he disliked intensely and considered a malingerer, was a Jew, and it is around the period of 1886–7 that the first signs of antisemitism appear in his correspondence. Some years later, Huysmans would side with the antidreyfusards, while Zola was to take the side of Alfred Dreyfus, a Jewish military man accused of treason (for more discussion of the affair, see Chapter Seven). Though Huysmans did not publish anything against Dreyfus, he made numerous remarks to friends about what he saw as Dreyfus' treachery. The political disagreements between Zola and Huysmans, in addition to growing artistic and personal differences, would lead in time to an end to their friendship. For the time being, he merely voiced his feelings about Zola to a few close friends, explaining that he had begun to draw away from naturalism. In 1886 he wrote to Prins:

> Basically in any case, I have drawn back from all labels. In any genre there are those who have talent, and those who have none; that is all there is to it . . .
>
> You can add to that an immense difference between Zola's ideas and mine, for example. He likes his period and celebrates it. I abhor it, and yet we manage to describe the same things.

If one looks into the matter, he is, all things considered, a materialist. I am not; basically I am in favour of the art of dreams as much as of the art of reality.[27]

Huysmans' discontent with Zola's theories and writings would soon give rise to a remarkable departure from naturalism in his next novel, as we shall see.

4

Descending into Darkness: *Là-bas*, the Abbé Boullan and the Occult

In 1887, after completing *En rade*, Huysmans searched for a topic for his next novel, but he felt uncertain of how exactly to proceed. He knew he wanted to write a book that would challenge the scientific determinism so prevalent in France at the time, and he was eager to find a new formula for the French novel, which he felt was mired in tedious descriptions of the everyday world. In his view, second-rate writers, influenced by Zola, were publishing dull novels about mediocre people. His two previous novels, *À rebours* and *En rade*, had already deviated from Zola's theories, but neither *À rebours*, with its portrayal of a solitary protagonist living in an artificial world, nor *En rade,* with its vision of disintegrating reality, seemed to offer a new direction for the novel as a genre.

What was needed, he believed, was a different way for the writer to depict reality – not just the gritty details of daily life, but the mystery that is also part of human existence: the inexplicable workings of the mind, inspiration, creativity and the supernatural. The writer Édouard Dujardin, reminiscing about Huysmans at that time, commented:

> I was amazed to see the importance he placed, not on religious matters but on what I would term things of mystery, on all that transcends the tangible and the rational. He would tell strange stories full of sorcery, esoterism and werewolves – and even satanism, concluding, after a long silence: 'It's very strange! . . . It's very strange!'[1]

In part, Huysmans' dissatisfaction with naturalism stemmed from his own anxiety concerning Anna Meunier's deteriorating health. Though at this point he still hoped she would recover, her mysterious illness defied her doctors' efforts to diagnose or cure it, and he was beginning to fear the worst. Despite the great strides being made in the biological sciences at this period, science was seemingly incapable of finding a way to help her. In addition, her medical expenses, all of which he paid, were a drain on his modest salary from the Ministry. The writer Léon Bloy wrote to a friend that he had spent the evening with Huysmans and witnessed the unimaginable:

> I have seen . . . something that I had never seen before, and that few people would think possible: I have seen the author of À rebours crying. Ah! He must have been truly in despair, for he is not at all like me and he does not cry easily. Human existence is really too unhappy! This terrible grief caused by the dangerous condition of his lover of twenty years is aggravated and exacerbated by almost insoluble financial problems.[2]

In the summer of 1888 Huysmans' state of nervous exhaustion was so severe that his doctor recommended he take a long trip to escape his troubles. Anna's health seemed to have stabilized temporarily, so, leaving her in the care of friends and family members, Huysmans went on vacation to Germany, meeting up with his friend Arij Prins, who lived in Hamburg. Travel brought him some peace of mind; the landscape and people of northern Germany appealed to his melancholy temperament, and he was planning to write a book about his travels. The friends' primary goal was to view the collections of Primitive paintings in the museums of Lübeck, Berlin, Hamburg and other northern German cities. From visits to the Louvre, Huysmans already knew and loved this school of painting, and he wanted to discover more about it. In Berlin he was entranced by Rogier van der Weyden's triptych of the Nativity, noting that it was like a prayer in paint.

But it was in a museum in Kassel that he discovered the painting that forever changed his life and aesthetic vision:

Matthias Grünewald's *Crucifixion*. When he first saw this work, he was overcome by awe, and it continued to haunt him after his return to Paris. What struck him was its extreme realism – including graphic details showing Christ's festering wounds – combined with an intense spirituality that transcended the physical degradation. Here, at last, was the answer to Huysmans' quest for a new approach to the novel: a formula he decided to call 'spiritual naturalism'. Convinced that no words could express this concept so well as Grünewald's painting, he determined to write an essay describing the work and explaining his theory. He had no idea at this point that this essay would become the opening chapter of his next novel, *Là-bas*, but he did know that, for him, this painting symbolized a new kind of writing.

Upon his return to Paris, Huysmans was distressed to find that Anna was now bedridden, and no longer able to make her customary weekly visits to his apartment. There was little time to write because he was busy arranging medical visits and treatments. Yet still he managed to begin two projects: a book on Germany, and a novel about eccentric people plotting to put a Bourbon king back on the French throne. This group, which actually existed, was called the Naundorffists.[3] It intrigued Huysmans because its members were deeply involved in occultist and spiritualist activities. He was getting interested in the occult himself and had met a number of Naundorff followers at the home of Charles Buet, a Catholic writer with whom he had become acquainted.

Overall, though, his main concern was Anna, and his despair over her worsening condition grew as winter set in. In late January 1889 he wrote peevishly to Prins that because Anna was sick and unable to do housekeeping for him, his apartment was in chaos; he was even obliged to mend his own clothing!

> As for my wife, it's still the same situation. The regular doctors can do nothing, so I'm having her treated by one of my good Parisian homeopaths. But it's the same thing. She no longer can leave her apartment. It has been a frightful mess for me. I have to sew on my own trouser buttons, etc.[4]

Unfortunately, all his efforts to find a cure for Anna, including an unsuccessful attempt to have her examined by Dr Jean-Martin Charcot, the celebrated specialist in nervous disorders, proved fruitless. Charcot was no longer practising medicine, and the various remedies suggested by his colleagues did not help. The change in her was heartbreaking: in place of the gentle companion he had loved for almost twenty years, all that remained was an irrational invalid. It was clear to him not only that her physical paralysis was increasing, but she was losing her sanity.

Huysmans' concerns about Anna were not the only cause of his profound sadness and disgust with life. The political situation in France, with the emergence of General Boulanger as a contender for the Presidency of France, disturbed him, since his own civil service job depended upon the current government remaining in power. Huysmans and many other concerned citizens feared Boulanger would become a dictator if elected, but his opponents were not much better. France's moral decline was evident. He wrote to Prins: 'Here there is nothing any more – except the political disgust of the moment. A frightened city, blanketed with political posters, talking

Matthias Grünewald, *The Isenheim Altarpiece*, 1512–16, oil and tempera on limewood panels.

in favour of Boulanger or Jacques, exhausting itself with fist fights at political rallies, tearing itself apart in the press.'[5]

All this political turmoil and Anna's poor health made it difficult for Huysmans to make much progress on his novel, which he had decided to call *Là-bas* (Down There). However, a major event was about to take place in Paris that would capture his imagination and renew his creative powers: the Exposition Universelle of 1889.

There had been previous world's fairs in Paris, but this one marked the hundredth anniversary of the French Revolution, and it was far larger and more elaborate than any of the others. Although he was at first put off by the crowds of noisy tourists arriving to see the Exposition, Huysmans soon became enthusiastic. There were so many new and unusual events and exhibits: a group of alluring Javanese dancers, a model of a medieval alchemist's laboratory, and paintings by contemporary European artists. His own troubles were eclipsed by the excitement of this great event, and he began writing a series of articles about it, describing paintings by Stevens, Moreau, Whistler and Burne-Jones. He also wrote about the buildings and monuments constructed for the fair. One of his more remarkable essays is a scathing condemnation of the Eiffel Tower, the centrepiece of the Exposition, which he dismissed as 'a solitary suppository, riddled with holes'.[6] This collection of writings, along with some previously written articles on Degas, Rops and other modern artists, was published as a book entitled *Certains* (Certain Artists) in 1889. It was favourably received and sold rather well.

Encouraged by the relative success of *Certains*, and reinvigorated by the events and exhibits of the Exposition, Huysmans determined to focus all his energies on the partly written novel he had begun about the Naundorff cause. Part of his research for this novel involved an intensive study of alchemy and black magic, and as he read arcane books on these topics, he discovered the enigmatic figure of Gilles de Rais, a medieval child murderer who was also a fanatical alchemist and a soldier in Joan of Arc's army. To Huysmans, the opposing forces of good and evil seemed to be at odds within Gilles. How, he wondered, could this man be both a pious Catholic, willing to die for God and

France, and a sadistic paedophile who practised black magic? On an impulse, he decided to travel to Brittany to visit Gilles de Rais' castle of Tiffauges, where he poked around in the ruins, claiming he could still see the bones of Gilles' young victims – much to the horror of the friend who had accompanied him. Abruptly, upon his return to Paris, Huysmans made up his mind to shelve his unfinished novel. Instead, he would write a new novel focusing on Gilles de Rais and his descent into satanism. Despite the change of subject, its title remained the same: *Là-bas.*

Why was Huysmans so fascinated by satanism? Given his ecstatic response to the Grünewald painting of Christ on the Cross the year before, and his theory of spiritual naturalism, one might have expected him to choose a religious topic for his novel – the story of a martyr, perhaps. But Huysmans distrusted the Roman Catholic Church, viewing it as repressive and hostile to writers and artists. Since he longed to find an escape from the everyday world, writing about satanism appealed to him, as it offered an opportunity to explore a dark, hidden realm. The occult sciences, including magic, astrology, magnetism and what might be called the black arts, were very much in vogue in late nineteenth-century France. It was fashionable to attend seances and other spiritualist events, and Huysmans had several writer friends who were enthusiastic participants in such activities. In addition to his own curiosity about satanism, he knew the topic would scandalize critics and the reading public, and he knew that scandal would sell more copies of his book – a marketing technique he had learned from Zola.

Reading about cases of demonic possession and exorcism as he prepared his novel convinced Huysmans that he needed to meet an actual member of a satanic cult in order to understand why people believed such things. He had heard about the Abbé Joseph-Antoine Boullan, a defrocked priest who had been a celebrated exorcist and was later denounced as a heretic by the Catholic Church, and he resolved to contact him. There were rumours that this man had seduced women and preached heretical doctrines, but Boullan's shady reputation only made him more intriguing in Huysmans' eyes. His friend Berthe Courrière, who had contacts in occult circles,

J. A. Boullan, *c.* 1885.

gave him Boullan's address and Huysmans wrote to him, explaining that, for a novel he was writing, he needed accurate information about the existence of demonic cults in France:

> It happens that I'm weary of the ideas of my good friend, Zola, whose absolute positivism fills me with disgust. I'm just as weary of the system of Charcot, who has tried to convince me that demonianism was just an old wives' tale . . . What I want to do is to teach a lesson to all these people – to create a work of art of a supernatural realism, a spiritual naturalism. I want to show Zola, Charcot, the spiritualists, and the rest that nothing of the mysteries which surround us has been explained.[7]

After some hesitation, Boullan agreed to correspond with Huysmans. However, he denied being a satanist, claiming instead to be an ardent defender of the Church, eager to expose the dangers of such groups. These cults, he maintained, were spreading rapidly. Despite the unsavoury rumours surrounding Boullan and warnings from the Rosicrucian writers Stanislas de Guaita and Oswald Wirth, who claimed to have witnessed him engaging in immoral behaviour, Huysmans determined to meet and consult with Boullan, whom he viewed as a sort of 'white magician' battling the forces of evil. The two began a lively correspondence, and before long Huysmans was receiving daily packets of material from the renegade priest on topics ranging from magical remedies for demonic possession to medieval Devil worship. They became friends, though they did not meet until six months later, when Huysmans took his annual holiday in Lyon and visited Boullan.

Boullan's 'evidence' of the existence of satanism in contemporary France excited Huysmans. Writing to his friend Jules Destrée, he boasted: 'I've found a former priest, the only one who knows all about the occult sciences and true, authentic satanism. He's devoted to me and has put into my hands the most shocking documents that anyone has ever seen.'[8] Now he had a clear vision of his novel. Writing furiously, and inspired by the shocking material Boullan had sent, he completed half the novel in a few months.

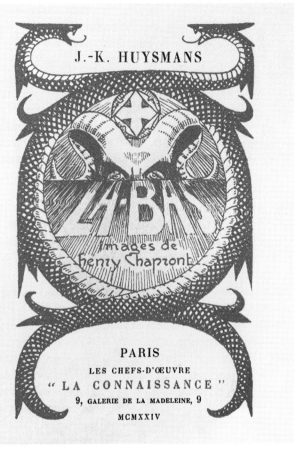

Title page of *Là-bas* (1924 edn).

Gone were his difficulties finding time and energy to write; gone as well his depression concerning Anna Meunier, though he continued to oversee her care. Perhaps because he was still influenced by naturalism, he had needed reassurance that his novel was based on true facts. The renegade priest was living proof of the novel's authenticity as an exposé of satanism – or so, at least, Huysmans believed.

In fact, Huysmans had been duped. Far from being a Christian crusader, Boullan was in reality a practitioner of heretical rituals involving sexual abuse, fraud and possibly infanticide. He had even spent time in prison. It was with good reason that the Church had expelled him from the priesthood. But Huysmans did not discover the truth until several years later. After Boullan's death in 1892, Huysmans inherited the ex-priest's private papers. It was while going through them that he discovered the 'Cahier rose', a confession written by Boullan, detailing a dizzying assortment of crimes.[9] Though by nature sceptical, Huysmans proved startlingly gullible where Boullan was concerned. The sheer volume of the material Boullan sent and the eloquence of his arguments convinced him that black magic and satanism were real.[10]

When *Là-bas* appeared in early 1891 in instalments in the magazine *L'Écho de Paris* and in book form a few months later, it was bizarre and disturbing – and immensely popular. Within a double time frame, the novel combines two narratives: the story of Gilles de Rais' grisly crimes in the fifteenth century, and the experiences of Durtal, a contemporary writer who is working on a book about Gilles.[11] As Durtal researches black magic for his book, he discovers to his surprise that demonic cults are alive and well in modern-day France. Erudite discussions on satanism are juxtaposed with details of Durtal's own life as the novel shifts from one time period to the other. Descriptions of succubi, satanic rituals and black masses are woven together with horrific accounts of Gilles de Rais' crimes. At times, since the crime sequences take place in Durtal's mind as he prepares to write his book, he seems almost to *become* Gilles de Rais – a puzzling and frightening development, as Durtal is to all appearances rather timid and retiring. In a key scene, he attends a black mass, but does not participate because the ritual disgusts him. A brief love affair with a female admirer provides short-lived romantic interest. As the affair ends, Durtal completes his novel and resumes his solitary existence.

The opening chapter of *Là-bas* stands apart from the rest of the book. A literary manifesto thinly disguised as a dialogue between

Durtal and his friend Des Hermies, it sets forth Huysmans' theory of spiritual naturalism, formulated after he discovered Grünewald's *Crucifixion* in Kassel. In the novel, it is Durtal who sees and is transfixed by the painting. Alone in his Paris apartment, he recalls the powerful emotions he felt when he first saw it, and in his mind's eye it appears before him: 'Durtal shivered on his sofa and half-closed his eyes in pain. Now that he had evoked it, he could see the painting there before him with an extraordinary lucidity.'[12]

A vivid, almost hallucinatory description of the painting, with its depiction of Christ's martyrdom, follows. Durtal reflects that God's love for mankind shines through the physical degradation of Christ's body, offering inspiration to the viewer:

From that ulcerated head emanated glimmers of light; a superhuman expression illuminated the gangrened flesh, the eclampsia of his features. This carcass spread out before one was that of a God.[13]

(De cette tête exulcérée filtraient des lueurs; une expression surhumaine illuminait l'effervescence des chairs, l'éclampsie des traits. Cette charogne éployée était celle d'un Dieu.)[14]

Writers should emulate Grünewald, Durtal decides; in order to capture true reality, they must depict both the physical and spiritual aspects of existence: 'The novel, if possible, should divide itself into two parts – albeit welded together or rather commingled as they are in life – that of the soul and that of the body, and concern itself with their relationship, their conflicts and their harmony.'[15]

Là-bas marks Huysmans' definitive break with Zola, who is dismissed in this opening chapter as a writer who has seen his day. Huysmans had misgivings; as the novel was about to appear in print he commented: 'I'm expecting to be ridiculed, to have an unpleasant exchange with Zola and to face general astonishment at such documents and such a subject.'[16] To his surprise, the book was an immediate bestseller. Bookshops could not stock enough copies: '*Là-bas* . . . is an enormous success . . . 4,000 copies have been sold in under a week . . . People here are talking about nothing but Gilles de Rais and black masses.'[17]

Though Huysmans called it a novel, *Là-bas* teeters on the brink between autobiography and fiction. Much of what the protagonist experiences parallels Huysmans' own life between 1887 and 1890. Not only do he and Durtal share an interest in Gilles de Rais and the occult, but both are writers and confirmed bachelors with a taste for arcane books and art. In fact, a painting in Durtal's apartment that plays a key role in the novel is identical to a painting by Joachim Patinir that Huysmans himself owned.[18] In the novel, Durtal has a love affair with a mysterious woman who sends him anonymous love letters; this character, Mme Chantelouve, was likely modelled after Henriette Maillat, with whom Huysmans had an affair several years before the publication of *Là-bas*.[19] Huysmans included a number of Henriette's love letters almost verbatim in *Là-bas*, apparently without her consent. Other characters in the novel are also based on real people. For instance, the character of Dr Johannès, a courageous priest who battles satanism, is by Huysmans' own account inspired by Boullan, who must have been pleased with this flattering portrait of himself. Another character, M. Chantelouve, is modelled after Charles Buet, a Catholic writer and Naundorffist. Given all these parallels between Durtal and Huysmans, it is difficult to determine exactly where Huysmans' identity ends and Durtal's begins. But Huysmans' life and personality were in many ways quite different from those of his protagonist. For instance, Huysmans was devoted for years to Anna Meunier and was fond of her children, while Durtal lives alone and seemingly has never had a lasting attachment to a woman. Interestingly, there is no character in *Là-bas* that even faintly resembles Anna. And while Durtal is a near-hermit, Huysmans had many friends and corresponded widely with writers, artists, old school chums and members of religious communities. Perhaps it would be safe to say that in this book Durtal represents one aspect of Huysmans: the writer searching for a new approach to the novel and for some kind of mystical escape. Durtal also exhibits a number of Huysmans' personal eccentricities: like his creator, he is excessively bookish, set in his ways, indecisive and anxious about almost everything.

Là-bas stands as one of the most significant novels of the French *fin-de-siècle*. If Huysmans had focused only on satanism, it would no doubt have a less important place in French literature; but it is much more than a novel about demonic rites. In setting forth the new doctrine of spiritual naturalism, it inspired other writers to turn away from Zola's naturalistic style of writing and pursue a more inward-turned type of fiction in which author and protagonist are closely linked.

Soon after *Là-bas* appeared, Huysmans complained of a variety of physical and nervous ailments. In all probability, these health problems were caused by the stress and anxiety of his prolonged immersion in the world of satanism and by his personal difficulties, but Boullan maintained that they were the result of invisible 'fluidic attacks' from hostile Rosicrucians who were angered by the book's revelations. He offered to defend Huysmans with charms, incantations and prayers. More surprisingly, he offered to take the author's suffering upon himself. In later years this notion of 'substitution', according to which a person of great virtue willingly suffers in place of another, less perfect person, became a central aspect of Huysmans' religious philosophy.

However, Boullan warned, Huysmans would have to endure some of the suffering himself, because it was heaven's will. A month later Boullan wrote that he and his associate Mme Thibault were working hard at taking on Huysmans' maladies: 'You have experienced about 1/100th of the suffering that they are trying to cause you. We are enduring 90/100th of it, by our calculations.'[20] Over time Huysmans came to believe that Stanislas de Guaita and other Rosicrucians were indeed trying to harm him by supernatural means. He looked to Boullan for protection, convinced that the former priest's vast knowledge of satanism made him a powerful ally.

But even as he worried about warding off demonic attacks, Huysmans was planning a new novel that was to lead him away from the occult and Boullan. He was about to embark on a spiritual journey into Christian mysticism. In order to free himself from the satanic world he had described in *Là-bas*, he envisioned a new work that would be a sort of antidote to *Là-bas*: a novel about a troubled man's search for God. He wrote to Prins in early 1891: 'I want to write a sort of *Là-haut* (Up There) now, a white book.'[21] Huysmans was not leading a particularly pure life at this point, despite his plans to write a spiritual novel. He was patronizing prostitutes, especially an alluring woman named Fernande. Much as he tried to remain chaste, he found himself unable to resist her charms. This was a difficult time for him; Anna was confused and often irrational. He felt tremendous guilt and shame at what he viewed as his own moral depravity. 'I have guano juice in my soul,' he wrote in his private journal.[22] Because he knew he needed spiritual guidance, he asked his friend Berthe Courrière to put him in touch with a Roman Catholic priest. She introduced him to the Abbé Arthur Mugnier, who she thought would be a suitable confidant because he was an enthusiastic admirer of George Sand and other famous writers of the period. Mugnier had never read any of Huysmans' novels but was intrigued at the thought of meeting a writer and agreed to counsel him. At their first meeting, in May 1891, Huysmans asked a now-famous question: 'Do you have any chlorine for my soul?'[23]

The Abbé was a pious, down-to-earth man who enjoyed socializing with artists and men of letters. Huysmans liked him but found him rather uninspiring. Although Mugnier was gentle and patient, telling Huysmans that, in time, he would find the answers to his spiritual questions, he was not interested in long discussions on mystical topics. But Huysmans craved them. Consequently, even while meeting regularly with Mugnier, he continued to consult Boullan, whom he considered a great scholar of mysticism. Boullan, upon learning that his protégé was in touch with a Catholic priest, sensed that he now had a rival; he professed to be extremely concerned with Huysmans' physical and spiritual well-being and wrote him long letters full of sanctimonious advice. Perhaps in order to maintain his influence over Huysmans, Boullan claimed that he and Mme Thibault were still intervening to protect him from fluidic attacks. In early 1891 Boullan wrote to Huysmans from Lyon:

You have solid, true, honest friends here. Lean on us; for until the end, when the struggle is over, we will be able to lessen part of the suffering that heaven has reserved for you, but it is heaven's will that you should endure some of it yourself. – Why? Because heaven is planning great Blessings for you, and for what it pleases Heaven to give to us, we must pay for.[24]

Although Huysmans' reply to Boullan is unknown, one can surmise that he did not refuse Boullan's offer of help. As we have seen, according to Boullan, Huysmans' physical ailments were the result of spells sent by the Rosicrucians De Guaita and Wirth. Did Huysmans feel that his ailments had greatly improved as a result of Boullan's efforts? We do not know. Oddly, he does not seem to have noticed that Boullan seemingly contradicted himself, asserting that heaven had sent his maladies, and then claiming that the Rosicrucians were responsible. De Guaita and Wirth were the same two men who had tried to advise Huysmans against associating with Boullan, and who warned him that the ex-priest was disreputable. As it turned out, they were right.

In subsequent letters Boullan grandly assured Huysmans that *Là-bas*, by exposing satanic activity in contemporary France, had won him God's approval and forgiveness: 'Your Book has earned you a Pardon for your past. There has been absolution for the sins of your Life. Heaven wants to renew this Pardon for you, according to all the Laws of eternal catholic Dogma that you so admire in the Middle Ages.'[25] Despite his solemn words and authoritative tone, Boullan omitted a key concept of Roman Catholicism: a sinner cannot be pardoned for his sins until he repents and confesses. Huysmans had done neither. But of course, Boullan was no traditional Catholic.

Huysmans' high regard for Boullan led him to reveal the private grief that was tormenting him: Anna Meunier's incurable illness. He told Boullan of her advancing paralysis and insanity and he related his frustration at being unable to help her, despite consulting a myriad of distinguished medical experts. Perhaps he had some hope that Boullan, who claimed numerous miraculous cures to his credit, might be able to help her; but he surely was not prepared for Boullan's reaction. In a letter of 14 August 1891, the renegade priest declared he had known all about Anna's plight long before Huysmans had told him of it, but had kept his knowledge secret. The reason for his silence? Because since her illness was caused by occultist attacks aimed at punishing him, Huysmans himself was responsible for her impending death. In mid-August, Boullan wrote: 'This poor victim is suffering from an evil spell sent through black magic. But she was only stricken because of you.'[26] Surely he intended to shock Huysmans with this revelation.

Thus, in essence, Boullan maintained that by writing *Là-bas* and making enemies, Huysmans had inadvertently caused Anna's illness. Certainly he was aware of the additional anguish these assertions would cause. It would seem that he was deliberately manipulating Huysmans, attempting to make him feel guilty for his mistress's suffering in order to demoralize, since Anna's disease had begun well before he wrote *Là-bas*. In a further letter of summer 1891, the ex-priest deplored his own inability to help cure Anna but promised to pray for her to die peacefully. Curiously, he gave no explanation for being powerless to help her, despite his supposed successes in curing other hopeless cases. Instead he continued to insist that Huysmans was responsible for her illness. To make matters worse, Boullan also stated flatly that it was Huysmans' own sinful decision to take Anna as his mistress that had brought God's wrath upon her:

A Woman whom you decided to bring into your life is going to pay with her life, within a year, for having been in a relationship with you that was not in accordance with the divine rule. It is an expiation for her but you are the one being punished.[27]

One must wonder why Boullan was chastising Huysmans so vociferously. What did he want? Perhaps he hoped to force the novelist to adopt his own brand of heretical Catholicism. He warned Huysmans that he was responsible not only for Anna's ordeal, but for the torments of those who were suffering in his place: namely

Boullan and his associate Mme Thibault. If Huysmans did not cease being a sinner and convert, the ex-priest admonished, he would endanger all those trying to help him. It is ironic that Boullan, whose 'religious' practices included sexual abuse of women, should take such a moralizing tone with Huysmans, whose offence was entering into a relationship with a woman he loved.

Fortunately for Huysmans, at this point in his life he had another spiritual counsellor, the Abbé Mugnier, who was offering him hope and forgiveness, and he was already beginning to move slowly but surely towards a return to the Church. One month earlier he had made a religious retreat at the shrine of La Salette, where he had experienced some fleeting moments of transcendence. Soon his relationship with Boullan would come to an end.

5

The Spiritual Journey Begins: Religious Retreats and Huysmans' Conversion

After completing *Là-bas*, Huysmans went through a stressful, disconcerting period as he began planning his next novel. Although it was typical for him to be sad as he finished a book, this time his mood was darker. Writing *Là-bas* had drained him mentally and physically. Intense study of satanism, although he had tried to turn away from the subject, had a lasting effect on him, leaving him anxious, depressed and suffering from a variety of physical ills. As we have seen in the previous chapter, he was now in touch with a Roman Catholic priest, the Abbé Mugnier, to whom he had appealed in desperation for comfort and religious guidance. He kept his spiritual and psychological torment secret from all but his closest friends, claiming to everyone else that his visits to churches and monasteries were merely research for a new book portraying chastity and lust at war with one another. It was called *La Bataille charnelle*, though he eventually gave it another title: *En route*. The book's protagonist was once again Durtal, the main character of *Là-bas*, who has become disgusted with his sinful life and turns to Christian mysticism for relief. A similar conflict was going on within Huysmans himself, for despite his efforts to lead a chaste and virtuous life, he was compulsively visiting brothels and believed that he was being manipulated by diabolical forces. An image that he often used to describe his blackened soul was that of a cesspool or sewer. In a letter written early in January 1891 to his old friend Georges Landry, he frankly revealed his self-loathing: 'But what sort of phenol, what sort of cupric solution would clean out the great collector where the filth of the flesh gurgles away? It would take barrelfuls . . . a disinfecting thunderbolt . . . to correct the residual waters from the old drains.'[1]

Overcome by despair and disgust, he resolved to go on a monastic retreat. His short visit the previous summer to the isolated mountain shrine of La Salette near Grenoble had awakened a powerful religious yearning, marking the beginning of his transformation from secular cynic to devout Catholic. While there he had experienced both ecstasy and terror, and he had glimpsed another world that was pure and far removed from ordinary life. This is clear in a letter he wrote to Gustave Boucher:

> Imagine a plateau, surrounded by even higher mountains, above which gleam the eternal snows. At La Sallette [sic]   not a single tree, flowers die, birds are silent . . .
>
> The sadness of this plateau . . . is enough to make one weep . . . Vertigo and suffocation are all around. The sky is blocked by peaks, clouds pass through you. Below are frightful abysses, and one's head spins over them.[2]

Frightening though La Salette was to a man who had not seen much more of nature than the Jardin du Luxembourg, Huysmans discovered to his surprise that meditating quietly in a monk's cell brought him the greatest peace and contentment he had ever known. He described this discovery to Boucher:

> I ended up staying in my cell and that was really good, for it is the one place where one can really take stock of oneself. I spent some very sweet hours there, better even than in the church; but outside of the cell, in this solitude, walking like a prisoner within a confined space, bordered by the void, literally finished me off.[3]

Huysmans' retreat at La Salette transformed the course of his life and work. Its otherworldly atmosphere gave him new insights into himself and revealed the joys of spiritual reflection. Long after his return to Paris, the memory of La Salette continued to haunt him. A detailed description of it would appear years later in his novel

La Cathédrale. After his return to Paris, he longed to go on another monastic retreat; his job at the Ministry was tiresome and stressful, Anna's health was poor and *La Bataille charnelle* was not advancing as he had hoped.[4] Life in Paris seemed unreal and absurd. Without fully understanding why, he began buying up religious *objets d'art* and redecorating his flat on the rue de Sèvres in a bizarre blend of the sacred and the profane. Huysmans' apartments were always in some sense mirrors of his inner self, and the new decor revealed a dual longing for Christian consolation and decadent sensuality. Writing to Prins, he proudly described his freshly decorated abode, adorned with censers, copes and other religious objects: 'My apartment . . . has become rather peculiar . . . Since I needed to repair it, I had the whole place, including the ceilings, draped in pale garnet-coloured cloth. I threw in some pistachio-coloured furniture, and with all my church ornaments, it's rather nice.'[5]

Prins, unaware of Huysmans' spiritual yearnings, probably assumed his friend was decorating his apartment in the manner of Des Esseintes, the perverse protagonist of *À rebours*. After all, Des Esseintes had designed his bedroom to look like a monk's cell, while using only the most luxurious materials, thus mocking the very essence of monastic austerity. However, considering what Huysmans did next, it is evident that his new-found taste for religious objects was indicative of a genuine spiritual awakening. In fact, he was secretly planning to go on a long retreat to a monastery and convert to Catholicism there. When one considers that he had spent most of his life scorning the Church, the magnitude of his decision is clear.

Despite his determination to return to the Church, Huysmans knew that to do so would be difficult, for he was by nature indecisive and anxious. Because he felt unworthy, he dreaded the spiritual and psychological struggle that conversion to Catholicism would entail. For guidance, he turned to the Abbé Mugnier, asking where he might find a monastery that was less forbidding than La Salette, a place where he could confess his sins and return to the Catholic faith of his early childhood. Mugnier recommended a Trappist monastery, Notre-Dame d'Igny, hidden away in a verdant valley not far from Reims. Mugnier had just been there on a retreat himself and thought it would suit Huysmans because of the asceticism of the monks, who observed a strict rule of silence and self-denial. Encouraged by Mugnier's description of the monastery, he resolved to make a retreat there for nine days while on vacation from the Ministry. In June 1892, soon before leaving, he wrote nervously to Prins:

> I'm leaving for the monastery on July 12 . . . La Trappe is not pleasant, and I'm already trembling, but I absolutely need this, much more for my soul than for art. But I am very anxious about this solitude in a cell, with potatoes and cider as the only food – and the night services.
>
> In sum, I'm going through a crisis, with such strange things going on in my life since *Là-bas*, that there is nothing to do but let oneself be led.[6]

Prins, who was not particularly religious, now realized that his friend was not merely researching a new novel but going through a profound spiritual upheaval. As young men, the two had enjoyed drinking and womanizing together, and the change in his friend must have seemed strange indeed.

Full of misgivings, Huysmans set out for Notre-Dame d'Igny in early July 1892. He worried that he would be unable to tolerate the monastery's uncomfortable living conditions and strict routine of prayer, beginning each day at two o'clock in the morning. On the advice of the Abbé Mugnier, he had packed a little survival kit containing chocolate, tobacco and wine to make the stay easier. We have little direct information about Huysmans' first impressions of the monastery, but in *En route* Durtal goes on a retreat at a monastery that closely resembles Notre-Dame d'Igny. It is generally thought that Huysmans' own experience at Notre-Dame d'Igny was similar to Durtal's, though there is no way of knowing if he changed some aspects of the storyline.[7] In the novel, Durtal panics after the carriage that has brought him to the isolated monastery departs, leaving him standing alone at the door:

And with a swift feeling of dread, there passed before him the
terrible life of the Trappists; the body ill-nourished, exhausted
from the want of sleep, prostrate for hours on the pavement;
the soul trembling, squeezed like a sponge in the hand, drilled,
examined, ransacked, even to its smallest folds; and at the end of
its failure of an existence, thrown like a wreck against this rude
rock, into the silence of a prison, and the dreadful stillness of the
tomb! 'My God, my God, have pity on me!' said he, as he wiped
his brow.[8]

Durtal's fears vanish when an affable monk welcomes him and
shows him to his room. Serenity envelops him as he looks out the
window at the tranquil landscape of apple trees and fields of alfalfa.
Beyond them he can see a great white road disappearing into the
distance. This road, he senses, is symbolic of his own journey.

Less is known about Huysmans' actual experience at Notre-
Dame d'Igny. Letters he wrote to Prins and Mugnier indicate that
he was enthralled by the monastery and the Trappist monks,
who, despite their strict rule of silence and routine of near-
constant prayer, proved to be kind and rather indulgent. While
the spartan living conditions were difficult and the ambience was
intimidating, he felt uplifted. In the monastery guesthouse he
met a pious layman, Charles Rivière, an oblate who befriended
him, serving as a sort of mentor.[9] It was at Notre-Dame d'Igny
that Huysmans first began to think about becoming an oblate
himself. But despite his generally favourable first impressions, the
next few days at the monastery were fraught with trepidation, for
he dreaded having to go through confession – a necessary step
to returning to the Church. Although he had chosen to make his
first confession at a monastery because he had little respect for
ordinary priests, whom he considered too modern and worldly,
the thought of revealing his sins to an austere Trappist monk
apparently terrified him. While he seems not to have confided
his fears about this to anyone (except perhaps the Abbé Mugnier)
until after the ordeal was over, the description of Durtal's terror in
En route is so believable that one suspects Huysmans felt much the

same way: "'My God!" he said, all at once, "but I do not even know how a confession is made!"' . . . He stopped, and without any need of probing it his life sprang out in jets of filth.'[10]

There is a mystery surrounding Huysmans' fear of confession. What sins was he afraid to reveal? This matter will likely never be fully resolved. Although there are possible clues in *En route*, where Durtal confesses to certain sexual behaviours that he is ashamed of, one should not assume that Durtal is Huysmans himself. The author was far more complicated. In fact, in *En route* Durtal might best be seen as a caricature of Huysmans rather than a double. Although Huysmans had led a quiet, law-abiding life, we have seen that he was convinced he was morally corrupt. A study of his life and correspondence reveals three likely reasons for his shame and self-hatred: his deep involvement in the study of satanism as he wrote *Là-bas*; his long, out-of-wedlock relationship with Anna Meunier; and his compulsive patronage of houses of prostitution, where he indulged in a variety of sexual activities. It is helpful to examine each in some detail, in order to better understand his views on morality, as he faced confession.

It appears that he believed his near-compulsive study of satanism while preparing and writing *Là-bas* had been in some way morally wrong. He told friends that he felt compelled to purify himself by writing a spiritually cleansing 'white book'. The Abbé Mugnier, describing their first meeting, recalled that Huysmans said he felt sullied after writing *Là-bas* and wanted to make amends with a new book: 'He wanted to write a book that would be the opposite of *Là-bas*. But in order to do this he needed to transform himself morally: to *bleach* himself. That was his expression.'[11]

Huysmans never explained exactly why he felt impure after writing *Là-bas*. Perhaps he believed he had taken too much pleasure in learning about the Devil's dark practices, though publicly he maintained that the book was intended to warn and protect its readers against the dangers of contemporary followers of Satan. Enthusiastic study of satanism may not have been the only reason for his feelings of guilt. Had he actually participated in black magic with Boullan? The defrocked priest often conducted occult rituals with the intent of harming his enemies, but there is little clear evidence that Huysmans was actively involved, though he did observe and describe several of these rituals to friends. Like Durtal, he may well have attended a black mass. Though most critics doubt this, a passage in *Là-bas* describing Durtal's experience at a black mass is so vivid and detailed that it is hard not to think the author was present at such an event. While the Abbé Mugnier later claimed that Huysmans had never attended a black mass, his assertion is suspect. Huysmans' old friend and colleague Léon Hennique stated that Huysmans told him about attending a black mass. Baldick considers Hennique a more reliable source of information than the overly protective Mugnier.[12]

A second possible explanation for Huysmans' feelings of guilt is his long relationship outside of marriage with Anna Meunier. Even though he loved Anna, supported her and her children financially, and made sure that she was properly cared for until she died, Huysmans apparently never considered marrying her. This was probably due in part to the class difference between them. Even though Huysmans claimed to despise bourgeois values and often mocked them in his novels, he was himself a member of this class and had absorbed many of its prejudices. (When his good friend Villiers de l'Isle-Adam married his working-class mistress as he was dying in order to legitimize their son, Huysmans considered their union to be a terrible humiliation for the famous writer – even though he had helped to convince Villiers that it was necessary for the welfare of the boy.) His unwillingness to marry Anna may also have been caused by a deep distrust of the institution of marriage itself; like many artists and writers of the time, he was convinced that marriage was an absurdity, a concession to bourgeois norms, and that it invariably led to unhappiness. This attitude is evident in *En ménage* and *En rade*, novels in which the male protagonists are disillusioned with marriage. But as Huysmans became an increasingly devout Catholic, he surely felt some remorse at having caused Anna to live in sin, especially as it became apparent that her illness would prove fatal. Yet even though she was still alive at the time of his conversion, he made no effort to legitimize their relationship. It is significant that the author's clergyman friends scrupulously avoided mentioning Anna in their memoirs about him, presumably because they wanted to protect his reputation as a devoutly Catholic writer. This suggests that Huysmans himself may have been ashamed of his relationship with her once he returned to the Church and may have been reluctant to reveal it during confession.

If his profound interest in satanism and his failure to marry Anna are possible explanations for his fear of confession, there is yet another possibility: his visits to prostitutes. These visits had increased during the period when he wrote and published *Là-bas*. In his previously cited letter to Landry comparing his soul to a cesspool, he spoke of his 'filth of the flesh' ('mes saletés charnelles').[13] Prior to converting he had bragged to friends about his sexual exploits with prostitutes, but now that he was about to return to the Church, he may have viewed his fondness for certain sexual practices such as oral and anal sex as sinful. Though there are few documents other than the letter to Landry in which he expresses feelings of disgust concerning his sexual behaviour, in *En route* there are several passages describing Durtal's revulsion and remorse after visiting a brothel. But did Huysmans feel the same way? During the best years of his relationship with Anna, his visits to prostitutes had diminished, but when she became seriously ill, he resumed his patronage of a *maison close* with the rustic name of *La Botte de paille* (The Bale of Hay). He had consorted with many prostitutes over the years, but in 1891 a sultry sex worker named Fernande was his special favourite, and it was only when she left Paris with a rich American in the autumn of that year that the relationship ended. In September 1891, less than a year before his conversion, he still seemed unremorseful when he spoke about Fernande in a letter to Prins, with whom he was generally quite frank:

As far as filth is concerned, I have problems! I had discovered a
girl whose depravity was first-rate; she had managed to get it into
my blood and we had some fine times between us. Her delicious
and terrifying anus haunted me. I devoured it without respite
and now some American swine has deprived me of her. He is
carrying her off to run a bar in Cincinnati![14]

In contrast, Durtal's feelings in *En route* about the prostitute
Florence, who is in all likelihood modelled after Fernande, are
extremely negative. In the novel, Durtal is overcome by shame,
disgust and despair after each encounter with Florence but is unable
to stay away, for he cannot stop thinking about her; one gets a sense
of Fernande's 'delicious filth' ('délicieuses immondices') in this
passage from the novel:[15]

> Ah, that Florence – and he thought of a woman to whose
> vagaries he was riveted – continues to walk about in my brain.
> I see her behind the lowered curtain [she undresses behind
> the lowered curtain of my eyes], and when I think of her I am a
> terrible coward . . .
>
> He hated, despised, and even cursed her, but the madness
> of his illusions [the madness of her impostures] excited him;
> he left her disgusted with her and with himself. He swore he
> would never see her again but did not keep his resolve [He
> had to admit that no other woman knew how to prepare such
> delicious filth].[16]

The difference between Durtal's and Huysmans' attitudes towards
the prostitute is noteworthy. Since Huysmans' letter to Prins was
written only nine months before his conversion, it seems doubtful
that his favourable feelings about Fernande could have changed so
quickly as to mirror Durtal's hatred and disgust. In *En route*, Durtal
blames the woman for drawing him into 'aberrant' sexual practices
against his will; yet in Huysmans' letter to Prins, it is clear that his
sexual relations with Fernande were consensual. Surely Huysmans
was aware of the absurdity of Durtal's blaming a paid sex worker

for her attentions. It is probable that the novelist wanted the reader to notice Durtal's obtuseness and be amused by it. And yet Huysmans himself seems to have been equally obtuse at times where Fernande was concerned, for example implying in his letter that she enjoyed their encounters as much as he did – even though pleasing a customer was her job. While Durtal sees Florence as demonic and feels victimized by her, Huysmans seems fond of Fernande and does not view her as evil, but rather as a valued sexual partner. He may also have exaggerated Durtal's negative feelings in order to dramatize the struggle between lust and chastity. He was experiencing that conflict himself, though with considerably less remorse. He wrote to Boucher in late summer 1891: 'After exemplary behaviour on my travels, once back in Paris I was taken with an itch for filth, and I have spent long periods inside Fernande's spicy incense-burner. All this is very mediocre and not very proper, but it is very good, I must admit.'[17]

In sum, unless he drastically altered his moral views in the space of a year, Huysmans does not seem to have considered his fondness for prostitutes as much more than a sin of overindulgence. Perhaps his guilty conscience and fear of confession can be explained by all three of these perceived shortcomings: his fascination with satanism; his long, out-of-wedlock relationship with Anna Meunier; and his fondness for sex with prostitutes. Because it is so easy to slip into the assumption that Durtal's feelings are also Huysmans', it is useful to reiterate that Durtal is a fictional character created by a masterful writer who did not reveal all aspects of himself in his novels. It would likely be a mistake to think that the sole cause of the author's shame and self-hatred was his sexual behaviour, though this has been a common assumption made by readers.[18]

Despite Huysmans' extreme reluctance to confess his sins, he was determined to take this difficult step in order to feel cleansed, take communion and complete *En route*, his 'white book'. After a harrowing night at Notre-Dame d'Igny, during which he was so tormented by diabolical dreams that he considered suicide, he pulled himself together and managed to go through confession.[19] Soon after he wrote to the Abbé Mugnier:

> I have come through the hardest moment of my life – confession. It is done. I have been liquidated – I received communion this morning at the Abbot Dom Augustin's mass, and I am writing to you in grips of an infinite sadness, the idea of absolute unworthiness of a badly repaired soul, that has given all it could, but which needs to be propped up . . .
>
> But all the same, coward as I am, I wonder that I managed to come through this extraction. The forceps hurt me, but at last it is over.[20]

After his confession Huysmans began to feel joy and relief. Although at the Château de Lourps he had experienced an interlude during which he rejoiced in nature, he resumed professing hatred for it once he was back in Paris. But after his conversion he was able to revel in the beauty of the tranquil monastery grounds, taking solitary walks along the avenue of stately oak trees, praying and meditating. A swan gliding on the surface of a pond seemed to him a symbol of purity and hope. In some mysterious way, his changed attitude to nature was the result of his conversion. Now he took pleasure in contemplating the trees, animals and birds he saw around him, telling Mugnier: 'All in all, I am perfectly happy . . . I pray, meditate, smoke, dream by the edge of the pool, walk up and down the tree-lined paths, and am taking a cure in silence and fresh air.'[21]

In his previous novels, nature is either largely absent, or perverted and blighted, but in *En route* a sort of pantheism emerges. After making his confession, Durtal walks around the monastery grounds, rejoicing in the natural world:

> His vision of nature was modified; the surroundings were transformed; the fog of sadness which visited them vanished; the sudden clearness of his soul was repeated in its surroundings . . . These alleys, this wood, through which he had wandered so

much, which he began to know in all their windings, and in every corner, began to appear to him in a new aspect. A restrained joy, a repressed gladness emanated from this site.[22]

This new sense of unity with nature is evident in Huysmans' fiction written after his conversion, from *En route* to his final works.

By his own account, Huysmans' experience at Notre-Dame d'Igny was humbling and life-changing. It confirmed his sense that only in or near a monastery could he find true consolation and peace. For the rest of his days he believed this holy place was the epitome of medieval monasticism. On 8 August 1892, shortly after his stay there, he wrote to Prins:

> And what about the monastery, you say? It is a delightful and yet frightening place! Life there is more than hard. My soul has been shattered by it. One gets up at half-past two in the morning; perpetual silence; a dinner consisting of watery soup with oil added, an egg, a dish of vegetables with oil . . . but all the same, there are some exquisite moments. Anyone who talks about mysticism without having experienced this life does not know what he is talking about, and I would add that anyone who has not witnessed Trappist prayer does not know what prayer is.[23]

Still, much as he admired the monks of Notre-Dame d'Igny and appreciated the beauty of the services, Huysmans reluctantly decided that the rigorous routine of prayer, the poor quality of the food and the uncomfortable lodgings would ruin his health if he lived there. Back in Paris, he wondered if he would ever find a refuge offering him lasting inner peace. But he was beginning to change his life. At the end of 1892 he wrote to Charles Rivière, the oblate he had met at Notre-Dame d'Igny with whom he had formed a lasting friendship:

> Perhaps you and Fr Léon might have thought some morning of the penitent who dropped like a meteorite into your isolation, and in all charity, did you not wonder if he had gone under again?

Alas, he is evidently not of great worth, and has no reason to be very proud of himself; but after all, the bit of ground he has won over his habitual faults is thanks to you all . . . I have taken away with me from your monastery something resembling a powerful cordial of which a few drops suffice to set me on my feet again as soon as I feel myself going under.[24]

Over the next six years he would continue to seek out monasteries as refuges and sources of inspiration, always looking for one that perfectly suited him, where he could spend the rest of his life. That search would lead to several disappointments before he found what he was looking for.

6

In Search of a Monastery:
The Road to Ligugé

Upon returning to Paris in late summer 1892 after his retreat at the
Trappist monastery and a brief visit to Boullan in Lyon, Huysmans
was disappointed to find that he was neither happy nor at peace.
His life in Paris and his job at the Ministry seemed meaningless,
and the City of Light that had once fascinated and inspired him now
struck him as a morass of sin and temptation. He thought longingly
of the tranquillity and joy he had felt at Notre-Dame d'Igny and
yearned to go there again. But so long as Anna was alive, he felt
compelled to live in Paris to assure her well-being. He was trapped
in a life where no lasting happiness seemed possible, at least while
Anna needed him. Her mental state continued to decline, and
because of her bizarre behaviour she had been evicted from several
different apartments, forcing him to move her to new lodgings. Her
two young daughters had left home and were living with relatives.
This unhappy situation lasted well into 1893. He lamented to Prins
on 3 April 1893: 'I still have my poor mad woman on my hands and
should not decide on anything while she is still in this world. Then
I still have five years to go at the office before my retirement and I
have my book to write!'[1]

Not long after his stay at Notre-Dame d'Igny, as he reflected on
where his spiritual journey might lead, he decided that he needed
another religious mentor and confessor in addition to the Abbé
Mugnier. Exactly why he felt he could not choose Mugnier as
confessor is unclear. Although he and Mugnier had become good
friends and Huysmans looked to the priest for spiritual advice, he
may have thought that Mugnier was too worldly and overfond of

Parisian high society, where he was a popular guest and lecturer. Perhaps Huysmans, ever the mystic, also found his friend a bit too logical and rational. One day he impulsively decided to go to the church of Saint-Sulpice and leave the choice of confessor up to God. Whether by sheer chance or by God's design (as Huysmans believed), the priest on duty at the time, Gabriel Ferret, had long noted Huysmans' frequent visits to the church and was overjoyed to at last meet the famous author and guide him spiritually. Thus began yet another of Huysmans' many close friendships with men of the cloth. If Mugnier was hurt by the writer's failure to choose him as confessor, he never let on and the matter seems not to have caused any friction between them. Mugnier may well have been relieved to have some help from a colleague in managing this complex and troubled convert. Mugnier remained a close confidant and loyal supporter, as did Ferret. Mugnier was to outlive Huysmans by many years and wrote a book describing their friendship, while Ferret died at the young age of 44.[2]

It might be assumed that after his stay at Notre-Dame d'Igny, Huysmans would have distanced himself from Boullan, whose religious views had been declared heretical by the Church; but in fact he continued to stay in frequent touch with the defrocked priest. He still admired Boullan as a 'great mystic' who had been treated unfairly by the conservative Catholic hierarchy. He had begun to see that some of Boullan's eccentric beliefs were rather silly, but he continued to rely on Boullan as a supreme expert on mystical theology and the supernatural, and as a friend and mentor whom he could consult as he wrote *En route* (at this point still entitled *La Bataille charnelle*). When Boullan came to Paris on business in late 1892, the two men spent considerable time together discussing Huysmans' novel and Boullan's activities. It was to be the last time they would see each other.

In early 1893 Huysmans received shocking news: Boullan had suddenly died, under mysterious circumstances. Only days before his death the ex-priest had written that he was being assailed by demonic attacks. The next morning he wrote again to Huysmans, describing his ordeal: 'last night, a terrible accident occurred.

At three o'clock in the morning, I woke up suffocating. I cried out twice "Madame Thibault, I can't breathe", and when she came to me, I had lost consciousness. From three o'clock to half past three, I was between life and death.'[3]

One day later Boullan was dead. Although the symptoms he had described suggest a heart attack or stroke, Huysmans was convinced that his friend had been murdered by black magic. He and other admirers of Boullan publicly accused Boullan's enemies Stanislas de Guaita and Sâr Joséphin Péladan of having used demonic spells to kill Boullan, citing the latter's letter as proof. An article in *Le Figaro* on 10 January quoted Huysmans and the writer Jules Bois as declaring: 'It is incontestable that Guaita and Péladan practise black magic daily. That poor Boullan was in a perpetual struggle with evil spirits that they kept sending from Paris . . . It is quite possible that our poor friend Boullan succumbed to a deadly spell.'[4]

In the same interview Huysmans accused De Guaita and Péladan of waging occult war against him as well, claiming that every night at midnight: 'I suffer fluidic fist blows to my face and head' ('je reçois sur le crâne et sur la face . . . des coups de poing fluidiques'). As evidence that the attacks were not merely a figment of his imagination, he noted that his cat was suffering similar nightly torments. This rather preposterous affair quickly escalated, and it was not long before De Guaita, outraged by the accusations, challenged Huysmans to a duel. Initially, Huysmans accepted the challenge, but the threat of death or injury quickly brought him to his senses, and he arranged to settle the matter by publicly retracting his statements. For the rest of his life, however, he remained convinced that De Guaita had caused Boullan's death by long-distance black magic.

Although Boullan had named him as executor of his will, Huysmans was unable to attend his friend's funeral in Lyon or even to go there later that year, because Anna's worsening condition demanded his full attention. In April 1893 Huysmans reluctantly resolved to have her committed to the Sainte Anne psychiatric hospital. It was a shattering experience: Anna, who did not understand where she was going, insisted on taking great pains to dress up in her best clothes, causing Huysmans to feel intense grief and guilt. Soon after he had taken her to Sainte Anne's, he wrote to Prins that this had been the most painful moment of his life:

> It was horrible. She is suffering from general paralysis, raving, but not so mad as not to know where she is and to suffer atrociously. I went to see her yesterday, Sunday. I came away feeling sick. It is really awful. Imagine a room with 200 mad women singing and crying. The unfortunate woman you have asked to see is led into this flock, around which nurses run like sheepdogs; she arrives, unsteady on her feet, bursts into tears, and begs you to take her away. My heart breaks in advance when I think that on Sundays now I shall go and console this poor girl!
>
> Life is decidedly terrible; and woman is the most powerful instrument of pain that is given to us – whoever she may be![5]

Seeing Anna regularly in the asylum was torture for Huysmans. When he was unable to visit her, his faithful housekeeper, Mme Giraud, went in his stead. Painful though it was to see his beloved Anna institutionalized, it meant that he was now free to leave Paris more often, knowing that she was safely supervised. He kept up a busy correspondence with friends and colleagues, including a number of priests and nuns. The catastrophic events of the first half of 1893 – Boullan's sudden death and Anna's institutionalization – had an effect on his writing. One month after Anna entered the asylum, Huysmans abruptly discarded the substantial manuscript of his partly written novel *La Bataille charnelle* and began over again with a new focus and a new title: *En route*. He never explained his reasons for this change of plan, telling Prins simply:

> I am, for my part, more and more annoyed. I had written the greater part of my book, the length of a normal book, and I've just tossed it out. It's hard to give up two years of work, but it wasn't going well, I wasn't happy. I'm back at work and I'm beginning over with different aims.

All this and the problems of this poor unhappy woman that I go to see in the insane asylum on Sundays has killed me. I'm going through a bad period; fortunately I'm hoping to have my vacation in a month or two, and then I'll leave to calm my soul at La Trappe, but I've got to get there first. It's not pleasant.[6]

The revised novel was quite different, though in both versions the protagonist, Durtal, is a fictionalized persona of Huysmans himself. Instead of telling the story of Durtal's spiritual awakening, based on Huysmans' retreat at La Salette, the new version depicts Durtal's experience at a monastery very much like Notre-Dame d'Igny. While the change of place from one religious shrine to another might not seem to be of great importance, it was deeply significant for Huysmans, since Notre-Dame d'Igny was the place where his new life as a Catholic began. A few months after committing Anna to the Sainte Anne asylum, as Huysmans worked on *En route*, he made a second retreat at Notre-Dame d'Igny, where he was overjoyed to see his favourite monks again; but he had already decided that he could never live there permanently. Where could he find a monastery that offered peace, inspiration and a degree of physical comfort? He could only put his trust in God and wait.

Despite his spiritual awakening, daily life continued much as before, as he soldiered on at the Ministry, a job he abhorred but could not afford to leave. Towards the end of 1893 he received an unexpected honour: the prestigious award of Chevalier de la Légion d'Honneur, in recognition of his many years of faithful government service. Glumly, he told friends that he found the award an annoyance, because it resulted in unwanted attention that took time away from his writing. He grumbled to Prins:

There's nothing new here . . . I'm being bombarded by congratulatory cards and letters for this unimportant award of a ribbon . . . I was obliged to lose my temper to get out of a banquet that was being planned in my honour! And I'm spending my life writing polite thank-you notes![7]

By December, while still working on *En route*, Huysmans had developed a new passion, Chartres Cathedral, telling Prins that he had fallen in love:

> Nothing new here, except that I have discovered the most exquisite medieval cathedral there is, at Chartres, a blonde, slim church with blue eyes. The last effort of the Gothic style, emaciated, no longer needing flesh and bone, desiring to be ethereal, to rise, like a soul, to heaven. I am in love with this basilica where, what is more, one finds the finest sculpted figures of the Middle Ages; and I can easily go there, for it is only three hours from Paris by express train.[8]

The following year it seemed that his prayers for a monastic refuge had been answered when he met an impressive Benedictine monk who had been given the task of restoring the ancient abbey of Saint-Wandrille, near Rouen. This young man, Dom Besse, was bursting with energy and enthusiasm and was determined to make Saint-Wandrille a world-renowned repository of Christian art and literature – a dream that captivated Huysmans, who had long wished for such a haven. The two men soon began discussing how Huysmans might assist with the project and eventually live there as a monk or oblate. Huysmans was overjoyed as he saw the perfect monastery he had longed for about to become a reality. As envisioned by Dom Besse, Saint-Wandrille, once restored, would be a glorious holy shrine where Catholic writers and artists could live, write and immerse themselves in a paradise of religious art, literature and music. In no time Huysmans had become an unofficial consultant to Dom Besse, making numerous trips to the abbey and helping with the plans for renovation. As he penned the final chapters of *En route*, he looked forward to an eventual move to Saint-Wandrille, where he would at last be able to live a life of peace, comfort and prayer. As he explained to Prins:

> You've asked what is my goal concerning St Wandrille. Basically I'd like to retire there. It's a community of Benedictines who

are very erudite and very intelligent, who are working on a wonderful history of the Middle Ages. They tell me: 'come to us as soon as you can, as an oblate'; that is, I would live independently of the monastery and be able to come and go whenever I wanted.[9]

Unfortunately, this dream was not destined to become reality. Dom Besse, though idealistic and well intentioned, proved to be wildly impractical, spending most of the budget he had been entrusted with in short order, with little actual restoration to show for it. In December 1894 his exasperated superiors removed Besse from his position and sent him off to an obscure abbey in Spain – much to Huysmans' astonishment and chagrin, for he knew nothing of his friend's profligacy and attributed his exile to infighting among the Benedictines. After learning of this calamity, he wrote despairingly to his friend Boucher, who had also hoped to live at Saint-Wandrille: 'I feel as if I'm falling apart. The future is darker than before, and the illusion of a refuge is fucked up. Who would have thought there would be nothing left standing in this bitch of an age!!'[10]

In a melancholy frame of mind, Huysmans faced the new year of 1895. The failure of Saint-Wandrille had deeply affected him, and there was worse to come. In February, after a long, terrible decline, Anna Meunier died. The funeral was small, limited to family members. We have no description of who attended, but certainly her two daughters were present, and likely Anna's sister Joséphine, a few cousins and, of course, Huysmans. Her death came as a relief to all concerned – especially to Huysmans, who had shouldered most of the psychological and financial burdens surrounding her care at the asylum. It is a mark of his strong moral character that after Anna's death he continued to assist her young daughters; he and François Coppée arranged for Antonine to join the ballet of the Paris Opera, where she later became a celebrated dancer under the name Antonine Meunier, and when Blanche got married later that year he assumed a paternal role, giving her away at the wedding and in all likelihood helping with the costs of the event.

Only weeks after Anna's death, *En route* was published, offering a welcome distraction from his grief. While it sold well and attracted a great deal of attention in the press, it proved, as he had anticipated, quite controversial, primarily because of passages that were critical of the Roman Catholic clergy. Some critics praised the book for its compelling depiction of Durtal's spiritual struggles and eventual conversion, but others accused Huysmans of maligning the Church and its priests. He was at once amused and exasperated by claims that he had not really converted at all and was cynically using religion to sell his book. Even his old friend Céard doubted that his conversion was anything more than temporary. The Abbé Mugnier staunchly defended Huysmans by giving public lectures arguing that the novelist was a sincere convert to Catholicism. There was also great debate over whether Durtal was in fact Huysmans himself, or a fictional character created by a hypocritical unbeliever. Thus a great deal of the controversy centred on whether the novel was or was not autobiographical, and on Huysmans' criticism of the clergy. It may seem surprising to readers today that so little attention was paid to this unusual novel's literary merit and experimental style, but at the time religious issues were a popular topic of debate in French society. The Abbé Mugnier's well-publicized public lectures defending Huysmans' sincerity and explaining the novel did much to quell the controversy and boost sales of the book. *En route* touched many readers with its moving portrayal of Durtal's spiritual pilgrimage, and Huysmans received many letters from grateful readers who had been inspired to return to the Church after reading it.

While the modern reader may find the novel somewhat tedious at times, especially the many long meandering passages describing Durtal's theological debates with himself, readers at the time found the book intellectually stimulating, as for instance this description of Durtal tormenting himself about the concept of Purgatory:

He entered once more on that halting dilemma which had so recently assailed the goodness of the Creator in regard to the sins of man. 'Purgatory is then exorbitant, for after all,' said he, 'God knew that man would yield to temptations; then why allow them, and above all why condemn them? Is that goodness, is that justice?'

'But it is a sophism,' cried Durtal, growing angry. 'God has left to every man his liberty; no one is tempted beyond his power. If in certain cases, he allows the seduction to overpass our means of resistance, it is to recall us to humility, to bring us back to Him by remorse, for other causes which we know not, which it is not His business to show us.'[11]

Although the book was popular, some members of the clergy were infuriated by its portrayal of secular priests as out of touch with God. On the other hand, it was lavish in its praise of monastic orders and their isolation from the temptations of worldly life.

Not long after the publication of *En route*, Huysmans (who seems to have attracted such people) met another member of a religious order with a grandiose plan for a unique monastery. This time it was an eccentric nun who was abbess of a small convent in southern France. She sent him a rambling letter praising *En route* and proposing that they work together to found a new order of Celestine monks. Huysmans misconstrued her intentions and somehow convinced himself that the new monastery would be a sort of Catholic artists' colony where writers and painters would live and work together, creating Christian art. Because this sort of retreat had long been his dream, he was immediately drawn in. Though he had never met the abbess, Mother Célestine, and knew little about her, he embraced the project, telling his friends that she was another St Teresa of Ávila. When he and Gustave Boucher visited the abbess at her convent, he was charmed by her and by the abbey, which was old and picturesque. He wrote excitedly to Prins:

I've just spent several days in the most delightful convent imaginable. It's at the foot of the Alps, with rows of poplars, rivers, complete solitude and worthy nuns falling over themselves to spoil me with delicious meals . . . The abbess is an elderly 70-year-old mystic who is crazy about En route.[12]

The fact that the abbess had read and admired *En route* – and the delicious food at her convent – doubtless played a role in Huysmans' favourable impressions, along with his conviction that Mother Célestine was a modern-day saint. But he had not fully grasped her plan.

Boucher, who was more of a realist than Huysmans, soon began to have doubts about Mother Célestine's sanity; but Huysmans continued to believe in her. He was convinced that a brand-new order that he was involved in planning would be well suited to his personal requirements, such as artistic freedom, good food and comfortable lodgings. Warning signs began to appear as Mother Célestine's letters became increasingly garbled; but Huysmans could not bring himself to abandon the project. By the end of 1895 he had to admit that he and Mother Célestine had very different visions of the new monastic order. When he discovered that she intended to make the proposed monastery into a kind of religious thermal spa offering Dr Kneipp's hydrotherapeutic treatments to paying guests, Huysmans was horrified.[13] The last straw came in the form of an enthusiastic letter from the abbess outlining her plan to train Huysmans, Boucher and their artist friends as hydrotherapeutic masseurs. Only then did he finally recognize that the whole venture had been doomed to failure from the beginning. In June 1896 he wrote to Boucher:

My friend, a hundred wagons loaded with broken stone are falling on me as I read a letter from our mother of Fiancey . . . She has founded her abbey, which she has named the Abbey Kneipp! Instead of being monks, we can have the task of giving massages and showers . . . To have dreamed about a monastery and then find oneself in a hydrotherapeutic business takes the cake![14]

Disappointed once again in his hopes of finding a monastery where he could be secure and happy, Huysmans began work on a new novel, *La Cathédrale*, visiting Chartres frequently and taking extensive notes on every aspect of the famous cathedral, which he described in letters to friends as a 'blue-eyed blond' ('une blonde aux yeux bleus'). Often he was accompanied by his friend and confessor the Abbé Ferret. Meanwhile, his job had become intolerable. An interim bureau chief whom he referred to disparagingly as 'the Jew' ('le Juif') was making his life miserable, he fumed, by refusing to give him the summer holiday dates he had requested. It was at this time in his life that antisemitic remarks began to appear in his correspondence. Dirty politics ('les cochonneries de la politique')[15] and extravagantly rich bankers were signs, he was convinced, that the whole of French society was in a catastrophic moral decline. Along with many other prominent public figures, he blamed the Jews for France's woes. In his opinion, French literature too had deteriorated, and new writers were producing trash. He had begun to lose the desire to write fiction, declaring that once *La Cathédrale* was finished, he wanted to live in a monastery and write about the lives of saints.

In fact, *La Cathédrale* is not precisely a novel, though Durtal is once again the main character. What makes the work different from the previous novels is that there is even less plot, and the protagonist is as much Chartres Cathedral itself as it is Durtal. Huysmans' love for this magnificent sanctuary is apparent on almost every page, in lavish and affectionate descriptions of the stained-glass windows, statues and soaring Gothic columns. For Durtal and Huysmans, Chartres Cathedral is the embodiment of the Virgin Mary: 'In short, with her complexion of stone and her windows, Our Lady of Chartres was a blonde with blue eyes. She was personified as a kind of pale fairy, as a tall and slender Virgin, with large blue eyes under lids of translucent rose.'[16]

Durtal, like Huysmans, is enraptured and obsessed by Chartres. As in *En route*, long, stream-of-consciousness passages abound. But the work is also an ardent hymn to Gothic architecture. Near the beginning we are treated to lush descriptions of dawn as seen through the stained-glass windows and dizzying visions of Gothic columns. As Durtal watches, the rising sun illuminates the cathedral windows and figures emerge from the shadows:

> A quarter of an hour passed without anything becoming more defined; then their true forms revealed themselves. In the centre of these swords, which were in fact blades of stained glass, figures stood out in broad daylight; everywhere, in the middle of each window with its pointed arch, bearded faces flamed, motionless in the fire and, as in the burning bush of Horeb where God shone before Moses, everywhere amid these thickets of flame, in her immutable attitude of imperious sweetness and melancholy grace, the Virgin appeared, mute and still, head covered with gold.[17]

Reading this work, one is filled with a sense of awe at the mystical beauty of Chartres Cathedral. Lyrical passages are mingled with scholarly detail, both historic and architectural. Reading *La Cathédrale* awakens a strong desire to visit the cathedral and experience its powerful magic. For years the book was sold there as a guidebook for tourists, though they likely found it rather heavy going compared to a *Guide Michelin*.

As he worked on *La Cathédrale,* Huysmans clung to the hope that he would some day leave Paris for good and seclude himself in a distant monastery. But the right refuge still eluded him. In autumn 1896 he and the Abbé Ferret visited the Benedictine monastery of Solesmes, near Le Mans. The notion of becoming an oblate increasingly appealed to him, and he and Ferret had often discussed the matter. Ferret hoped that this imposing monastery, with its emphasis on intellectual and artistic activity, would correspond to Huysmans' vision. During Huysmans' two-week stay at Solesmes, the abbot, Dom Delatte, pressured him to become an oblate there. Under the spell of the abbot's powerful personality and persuasive arguments, Huysmans finally agreed that he would come to live at the monastery once he had retired. Soon after returning home, however, he began to regret his promise.

For more than a year after his retreat at Solesmes, he was assailed by doubts, utterly unable to decide whether or not to enter the monastery as an oblate. His priest friends, especially the Abbé Ferret, urged him to honour his promise to Dom Delatte, and he too believed it was God's will. Yet still he hesitated to take the final step. His main concern was that the iron-willed Dom Delatte had made it clear he intended to read – and possibly revise – anything Huysmans wanted to publish once he entered the monastery. In February 1897 the writer confided his grave doubts to Prins:

> Being unable to publish anything without the abbot's permission is fine; and having to submit my books to be examined from a theological point of view is fine too; but for the abbot to have the right to change my sentences, and to muck about with my style – absolutely not![18]

Work-related concerns added to his distress; without warning, his superiors, who had for some time disapproved of his strong religious leanings, informed him that his political views were contrary to those of the current government, and pressed him to retire. This surprised and angered him. Certainly he hated his job and had complained about it for years, but he had planned on working for another year or two in order to be financially secure. Fortunately, he was able to strike a deal with a popular literary magazine, *L'Écho de Paris*, to publish weekly extracts of *La Cathédrale*, pending publication of the book. This gave him an extra income and he arranged to retire early in 1898. But he was overwrought and indecisive as he wondered what life would be like in retirement and what to do about his promise to Dom Delatte to enter Solesmes as an oblate. In the midst of all these worries, an unhappy but not unexpected event occurred: the Abbé Ferret, his close confidant and spiritual adviser, died after a long illness, leaving Huysmans feeling utterly lost. In September 1897, the day after Ferret's death, he told the abbess of the convent at Solesmes: 'He was everything: my father, my friend, my brother! . . . Alas, I counted on him to help me in so many ways!' ('Il était tout, le père, l'ami, le frère! . . . Hélas, je comptais sur lui pour m'aider en bien des choses!')[19] He voiced a similar sentiment to Boucher, telling him that without Ferret he felt unable to make a decision about Solesmes:

> For that [decision concerning Solesmes] one would need a clearheadedness that I don't have. I'm lying helpless in utter darkness, and it's at this very moment that my poor Ferret has left me.
>
> Obviously the only thing to do is pray and wait, but these additional tribulations do nothing to cheer up my already fearful and singularly weary life.[20]

Hoping to find an answer to his spiritual dilemma, Huysmans made several more trips to Solesmes between autumn 1897 and summer 1898 to meet with Dom Delatte and seek a solution to their

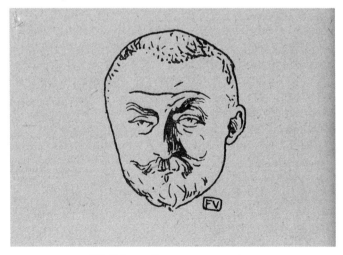

Félix Vallotton, *Huysmans*, c. 1898, woodcut.

Huysmans, *c.* 1900.

disagreements, but the inflexible abbot refused to change his stance. He urged Huysmans to make a leap of faith and enter the monastery without trying to negotiate the terms. Because Huysmans both admired and feared Dom Delatte, he was unable to stand up to him. His tendency to be swept away by powerful personalities led him to renew his promise to become an oblate in May 1898 – in spite of his grave reservations. Once again, it was a promise he immediately regretted. Finally, in July 1898, he made up his mind to abandon his hopes of becoming a Benedictine oblate. This decision was acutely painful. He wrote to Prins:

> I'm just back from the monastery, completely exhausted. I had a scene with the abbot of Solesmes, who wants to have me at any price, and I'm resolved now not to go there. In spite of everything, there are too many disagreements between us . . .

The abbot of Solesmes is a charming but terrible man. Fond of active mysticism, he crushes people, for their own good, it's true, but I don't have the courage to put up with such treatment at my age. I'm renouncing it all and for good. Here I am, back in the unknown, no longer knowing how to orient my life. In a word, I'm shattered.[21]

And so, for the third time, the dream of an ideal monastery had evaporated. The prospect of giving up his freedom as a writer was too daunting.

But in the midst of his despair and confusion, a new chapter in Huysmans' life was opening, though he did not yet realize it. New friends: a married couple, Léon and Marguerite Leclaire, became his devoted companions. They had been introduced to him by the Abbé Ferret, who had been spiritual adviser to all three. What surprised Huysmans' old companions Lucien Descaves and Gustave Boucher was that the Leclaires were well-to-do members of the bourgeoisie, exactly the kind of people he had always claimed to despise. Boucher and Descaves thought them dull and conventional, even pretentious. Although this negative view of the Leclaires has generally been accepted by scholars, the paradox no one has resolved is that, as we shall see, this was the couple with whom Huysmans hoped to spend the rest of his life. How can one explain his fondness for them? The fact that the Abbé Ferret had brought them together partly explains their bond, but there were other commonalities. Léon Leclaire, who had made a great deal of money in a family quarry business, was an intellectual with a passion for the natural sciences, architecture, gardening and photography. Since Huysmans had become fascinated by the religious symbolism of flowers and plants and was intrigued by nature and religious architecture, the two must have found ample common ground. Despite Boucher's low opinion of Léon Leclaire's efforts as an amateur photographer, Leclaire's perceptive photographs of Huysmans reveal much about the author's life during his later years. A favourable view of Leclaire was published in 1900 by the journalist Octave Uzanne, who described him as 'a man of science, very aware of all architectural matters, and of the art of gardens, especially interested in general chemistry, microbiology and amateur photography. At the same time, he is a fervently religious man who regularly attends services at the neighbouring abbey.'[22]

Like her husband, Marguerite Leclaire had an open mind, was eager to expand her knowledge of the world, and she was quietly pious. Uzanne wrote admiringly of her: 'A truly strong woman, with a lively intelligence about everything and open to all aspects of life. She is unostentatiously devoted to God, with no appearance of being sanctimonious or a provincial mystic.'[23] Thus according to Uzanne, who was a friend of Huysmans, the Leclaires were broad minded, keenly interested in a wide variety of subjects, and devout, non-judgemental Catholics. This would have meant that they were tolerant of Huysmans' often unorthodox style of Catholicism. It is not hard to understand why he enjoyed their company. Where Mme Leclaire was concerned, there was another bond; in addition to her intellectual interests and piety, she owned an embroidery shop. Anna Meunier had also been skilled in embroidery. Huysmans surely felt a certain nostalgic appreciation for this art and for the patient and expert blending of colours and textures that it requires.

Both M. and Mme Leclaire were younger than Huysmans and were apparently quite willing to cater to his many whims and eccentricities. Perhaps they felt it was their Christian duty to help their writer friend produce his religious-themed books, and he doubtless added a bit of adventure to their lives. One month after Ferret died, Huysmans impulsively made plans to travel to the town of Schiedam in the Netherlands to do research for a future book on St Lydwina of Schiedam, an obscure medieval mystic whose atrocious maladies fascinated him. The Leclaires faithfully followed him around while he visited museums and interviewed Protestant and Catholic clergymen about Lydwina. At one point Mme Leclaire accompanied him as he tried to track down a reputedly satanic priest, Louis Van Haecke, who had served as a model for the evil chanoine Docre in *Là-bas*. She and Huysmans lurked about in a church that the priest supposedly frequented and asked the parishioners pointed questions about him. Evidently she enjoyed this pursuit, though it proved fruitless. Perhaps the Leclaires filled a need in the solitary author for domesticity. Huysmans likely enjoyed the unthreatening feminine presence of the attractive and fashionable Mme Leclaire, who seems to have done her best to make him comfortable while protecting him from distractions, including pesky female admirers.

In fact, in the years following his conversion, Huysmans had his share of female admirers. Shortly before he made the decision not to enter Solesmes, a particularly troublesome fan, the Countess de Galoez, began pursuing him, showering him with letters and flowers in an attempt to seduce him. A scandalized Mme Leclaire tried unsuccessfully to deflect the woman's blatant advances. Huysmans jokingly nicknamed this person, who was Spanish, 'La Sol', and claimed to find her attentions merely annoying. But as her actions became more extravagant, he felt tempted to begin a liaison with her, despite his vow to swear off women. One may wonder why he continued to tolerate La Sol, who repeatedly appeared uninvited at his apartment. Was he flattered or intrigued? He told Prins that one evening he had found her at his door, swooning, and had brought her inside, fearing she was ill, whereupon she had spent the next hour on her knees, begging him to love her: 'What a woman! Bizarre, childish, overwhelming. She has the agitation of an unhappy little girl and the cunning of a badly behaved monkey. It's the temptation of Saint-Antoine . . . I resisted and all she got was an eternal *no*.'[24]

In the same letter, after calling her 'satanique', Huysmans admitted that he found her attractive:

She's a nice-looking woman – with a very pretty, supple body. She has a mobile face with irregular features and is not really pretty, but her eyes are like burning coals. She's an elegant dresser and not flashy. Whew! I'm very bothered by this adventure and don't know how it will end.[25]

Apparently Huysmans was still convinced that the Devil was actively interfering in his life, as evidenced by his description of La Sol in another letter as 'a brainless woman manipulated by evil powers and thrown across my path to prevent me from entering the monastery' ('une inconsciente mue par des puissances mauvaises et jetée sur ma route pour m'empêcher d'aller au cloître').[26] Despite having acknowledged and repented his sins, Huysmans still had a tendency to blame women for his own weaknesses. This tendency may even have worsened after the writing of *En route*, where he ironically depicts Durtal as unwilling to accept responsibility for his lustful behaviour. But Huysmans managed to remain chaste at a time when, because of Ferret's death and his painful decision not to become an oblate at Solesmes, he was vulnerable and felt he had lost his way spiritually. La Sol continued to pursue him until well into 1899, when she at last gave up her hopes of becoming his lover. He felt great relief when she finally disappeared and he was free of feminine entanglements. But there would be one more woman with an important role to play in his life, as we shall see.

As Huysmans struggled to ward off La Sol, he also had to deal with harsh criticism of *La Cathédrale*, which had appeared in bookshops in early 1898. To his surprise, it sold very well – better, in fact, than any of his previous novels. But there was considerable opposition from the conservative Catholic press, which had also been hostile to *En route*. While many lay readers were eager to obtain the book and hoped it would reveal more about Huysmans' own well-publicized spiritual odyssey, some members of the Catholic clergy made a concerted effort to discredit him. Despite the novel's glorification of Chartres Cathedral, the Virgin Mary and medieval Christianity, several prominent Catholic priests attacked it for its criticism of contemporary Catholic artists and writers, and for assertions that the secular Catholic clergy were too worldly. These were the same objections that these critics had made to *En route*. The worst blow occurred when they denounced him to Rome and the Index, claiming that his conversion was merely a publicity stunt and his religious devotion pure hypocrisy. Huysmans was outraged by these false accusations and took the step of writing a letter to the cardinal who was head of the Congregation of the Index, offering to remove any passages in the novel that were found to be offensive. As he had hoped, his letter, with its respectful tone, resulted in a decision in his favour, and the book was never placed on the Index.

Although he had turned his back on Solesmes, Huysmans had not abandoned his hopes of becoming an oblate. To escape his disappointment concerning Solesmes, he decided to take a holiday and pay a visit to Gustave Boucher, who had left Paris and was living in the village of Ligugé, near Poitiers. The trip was supposed to be a brief getaway, but Boucher had other ideas. He had been going through his own spiritual crisis and was aware of his friend's confusion and despair. Unbeknown to Huysmans, Boucher hoped to convince him to settle permanently in Ligugé. As part of his strategy, he contacted a number of clergymen in the nearby city of Poitiers and arranged for them to invite Huysmans to social and religious events. Upon his arrival, Huysmans was pleasantly surprised by the warm welcome he received. The little village of Ligugé struck him as peaceful and picturesque; most of all, he was delighted by the small Benedictine monastery of Saint-Martin de Ligugé. Both Boucher and the abbot of the monastery encouraged him to consider buying a house in the village. Some days into his visit, he noticed a building plot for sale on the edge of Ligugé. It was close to the monastery, an easy walk to the train station, and it was planted with fine, tall pine trees. On an impulse, he bought it for 3,000 francs and immediately began making plans to build a house. He told Prins:

> I've just bought a plot of land and I'm having a little house built. It's near the abbey, which allows me to be outside the monastery walls and retain some liberty to come and go, as well as freedom for my books. Living in this manner means I can dispense with the monk's robe and become a lay oblate.[27]

He went on to explain that living in Ligugé would be much less expensive than in Paris, and that now he would be able to live

LIGUGÉ (Vienne)
L'Abbaye St-Martin - Cloître (nord) et Autel Notre-Dame

Cloister at the abbey, Ligugé.

The abbey spire and cloisters.

exclusively on his book royalties and pension, rather than having to write articles for *L'Écho de Paris* to earn extra money. Moving to Ligugé would also leave him much more time to work in peace and quiet on his new book about St Lydwina.

In the same letter, he remarked: 'I'm building the foundations of a little colony of Benedictine oblates' ('[Je] jette les bases d'une petite colonie d'oblats Bénédictins'). This was another attempt at realizing his vision of a brotherhood of Catholic artists and writers living as oblates. It failed to materialize after a key potential member, the gifted young artist Charles Dulac, suddenly died. The hoped-for refuge near a monastery, however, was to become a reality – at least for a time.

Just what led the man who had been incapable of making decisions suddenly commit to living for the rest of his life in a village he knew little about and plan to become an oblate at a monastery he was unfamiliar with? After the disappointment of Solesmes, he was eager to find a new way to achieve his goal of ending his days in a religious haven, while at the same time retaining his artistic freedom. The fact that his good friend Boucher lived in Ligugé had much to do with it. In addition, another friend, Dom Besse, the impractical monk who had tried to restore Saint-Wandrille, was now at the Ligugé monastery. And the enthusiastic welcome offered by the clergy of Poitiers reassured him that he would find compatible religious companions nearby. Amid all the confusion and excitement of his new plans, he felt sure he was being led by God. Unlike the autocratic abbot of Solesmes, the head of the monastery of Saint-Martin was gentle and flexible, quite willing to allow him personal and artistic independence. Huysmans had read that this type of oblature had existed in the Middle Ages, when in addition to those living within a monastery there were also lay oblates who lived outside the monastery with which they were affiliated.

After purchasing the building lot, Huysmans quickly convinced the Leclaires to join him at Ligugé and share ownership of the house that was to be built, which he had already named the Maison Notre-Dame. It seems that their intent was mainly to

Huysmans with friends at Ligugé, *c.* 1901: (left to right) Léon Leclaire, Georges Rouault, Antonin Bourbon, Dom Besse, Paul Morisse and Huysmans.

support him as he sought to find a final home where he could worship and write; it would seem that they did not intend the house to be their sole residence, as they were frequently away travelling or in Paris. Ever solicitous of Huysmans' happiness, they left the design details for the Maison Notre-Dame up to him. Their financial backing allowed him to plan exactly the kind of house he desired. After many delays in the construction, the Maison Notre-Dame was completed at last, and in July 1899 Huysmans and the Leclaires moved in. The couple occupied the ground floor, while Huysmans lived in a suite of rooms upstairs. The house was rather grand – much more so than his previous apartments. An article in *L'Écho de Paris* gave the following description of it:

> This newly built house is brilliantly white, situated at the corner of an enclosed area planted with beautiful evergreen specimens . . . One gets there by a little path through the fairgrounds that leads to an iron gate with closed shutters. This simply designed limestone dwelling with a Romanesque Byzantine porch looks like a little religious community, a tiny brotherhood of mercy.

The house at Ligugé.

> This is indeed a close-knit community of affectionate
> friends, united in a life of quiet labour and illuminated by a
> mutual hope and faith.[28]

Building a new home and a new life raised Huysmans' spirits; he
wrote detailed letters to his friends, enthusiastically describing
the Maison Notre-Dame as it took shape. In addition to the house
itself, there was a chapel as well as an elaborately laid out liturgical
garden filled with symbolic herbs and flowers. The indecisive convert
had at last found a place where he could be at peace. Perhaps for
the first time in his life, he was truly happy. Life at the Maison
Notre-Dame was tranquil. Huysmans and the Leclaires spent time
together, attending religious services daily. Mme Leclaire oversaw the
household, keeping track of all the domestic details. Catholic artists
and writers often came to visit and these visits were recorded in Léon
Leclaire's photographs. A journalist who came to see Huysmans
observed that the once truculent and pessimistic novelist had been
transformed into a serenely happy retreatant. In March 1901, after
a suitable period of study and preparation, Huysmans became a
Benedictine oblate in a private ceremony, off limits to inquisitive

reporters. For the new oblate, little changed after that, for his life was already a satisfying blend of writing and prayer; each day he worked on his biography of St Lydwina and attended mass and vespers at the monastery. While living in Ligugé, he completed the book. When it was published in 1901, it did not attract a great deal of attention but was praised by several religious orders. From time to time he went to Paris to meet with his publisher and to convene the Académie Goncourt, of which he was the first president.[29] But he was always eager to return to his house in Ligugé. As he wrote contentedly to Prins in April 1900, he was immersed in reclusive bliss:

> I don't feel any desire to travel this year. I have masses of work to do and I'm so accustomed to my monastic services and to this semi-monastic life I'm leading that the thought of leaving it horrifies me.
>
> Obviously, it's quite monotonous, but at the same time it's so peaceful! I'm immersed in such marvellous works on the Middle Ages that I truly don't have time to be bored. Plus I have dinners at the monastery that give me a change from my own meals. And I take walks in the garden, which is very pretty, with old cedars and cypress and pines.[30]

Unfortunately, this tranquil existence that he had yearned for and finally achieved did not last long. Threatening developments on the French political horizon began to worsen, as the French government moved to secularize the country. Catholicism was under attack, and the first signs of trouble for Huysmans manifested themselves in the hostile behaviour of the citizens of Ligugé towards the monks. At first he hoped that the monastery could weather the crisis, but under President René Waldeck-Rousseau and his virulently anticlerical successor Émile Combes, laws imposing severe restrictions on religious orders forced many to leave France. As a result the monks at Ligugé made plans to leave for Belgium. Huysmans hoped that a few monks would remain at the Ligugé monastery, and that he could go on living in his house and attending services. But he was not being realistic. At the end of 1901, the last monks left for Belgium and he had to face the fact that his time at Ligugé had come to an end. He had only spent two years in the Maison Notre-Dame; in his mind, following the monks to Belgium was not a possibility. The only place to go was Paris, the city he loved and hated. However, he was not ready to live in an apartment as he had before, and was determined to stay temporarily in the guest rooms of a Benedictine convent on the rue Monsieur. Once again, he was in search of a monastery, but failing that, he needed an urban refuge.

Huysmans photographed by Dornac, *c.* 1893–5, his wall adorned with a crucifix.

7

The Final Years

From his window in the Maison Notre-Dame, Huysmans watched gloomily as the monks prepared to leave Ligugé in the summer of 1901. He knew that he too would have to leave, but where could he go? He was 'out of orbit' ('désorbité'), as he put it. In a letter to Prins, he lamented:

> The monks of Ligugé are probably going to leave France in November. Here I am again, dragging my arse, not really knowing what I'm going to do. Obviously, the simplest would be to go back to Paris to live, but it has become such an ignoble city, with its cars, its electric trams and the filthiness of the Métro.[1]

In spite of his negative feelings about contemporary Paris, Huysmans made up his mind to return there to live. He still had friends in Paris and looked forward to strolling along the Seine, visiting the Louvre and browsing through the used books sold by the *bouquinistes*. It was still the city where he had grown up and spent the greater part of his life, and he had once loved it passionately. But even after he had made this decision, he delayed his departure from Ligugé because he was reluctant to leave the Maison Notre-Dame and the monastery. In September 1901 he accompanied the abbot to the train station and said goodbye. The Leclaires had already begun preparing to depart from Ligugé, and the Maison Notre-Dame was being put up for sale. He wrote to Prins:

This very morning I saw off my father the abbot on the train. He was the last to leave . . . and now the bells no longer ring, and the clock that sounded the hours in the village from the top of the abbey tower has stopped. All is dead. The goodbyes this morning were heartbreaking.[2]

In late October Huysmans moved back to Paris and took up lodgings at the Benedictine convent on rue Monsieur, where he had been offered the use of a guest apartment. The rooms were quiet and the ambience was appropriately austere, but the place was frigid and damp. But he soon made a new friend: an elderly monk who lived upstairs and later became his confessor. At first, Huysmans tried to endure the physical discomfort and make the best of the situation, writing to Prins:

> I have finally moved in. The apartment, which is on the second floor, is dark and cold, but spacious, and the inconveniences are compensated by so many advantages that I don't dare complain . . . There is no kindly gesture that the Benedictine abbess has not shown me, and the services and medieval Gregorian chant are marvellous. And yet I don't feel truly settled. I feel as though I've got off at a way station, not the final destination.[3]

In spite of the abbess's efforts to make him comfortable, Huysmans decided after some months to move into a flat at 60 rue de Babylone, where he had more privacy and the rooms were warm and cheerful. The damp convent apartment, he suspected, had caused a number of ills, including rheumatism and toothache.

Even without the Leclaires, who had moved to Lourdes, he was not lonely; his old companions Descaves, Henri Girard and Landry visited him often, along with his newer clerical friends, including the Abbé Mugnier and various Benedictine monks. He was now hard at work on a new novel, *L'Oblat* (The Oblate of St Benedict), inspired by his own experiences at Ligugé. While he wondered how many readers would be interested in a book about the life of an oblate, he did not let the matter of readership deter him, warning all who showed an interest that the novel would be difficult and slow moving. Since *En route* and *La Cathédrale* had sold well, he hoped that *L'Oblat* would appeal to the same group of readers. These books had been successful, he was convinced, because many people were disgusted with the immorality and materialism of the times. In his rue de Babylone apartment, he was comfortable and content, working steadily on *L'Oblat*. In addition, he managed to produce a steady stream of articles for literary magazines in order to supplement his pension and meet the high expenses of living in Paris. While during his earlier years as a novelist he had found writing to be a struggle, it now came more easily, and the novel progressed rapidly. By late November 1902 he had only two more chapters left to compose and expected *L'Oblat* to be published early the next year.

In addition to the pervasive anticlericalism that had led to the expulsion of religious orders from France, antisemitism was also rampant. At the time of Huysmans' return to Paris, the Dreyfus Affair was rocking the very foundations of French society, dividing the nation into two hostile camps: those who believed Alfred Dreyfus, a Jewish officer accused of treason, to be innocent, and those convinced he was guilty.[4] The anti-Jewish sentiment permeating French institutions made it easy for the baseless accusations against the young captain to be believed, even after they had been discredited. Despite clear evidence that Dreyfus was blameless, Huysmans and a number of other Catholic writers, including Paul Valéry and Léon Daudet, sided with the antidreyfusards. His involvement in the controversy consisted mainly of negative remarks about Dreyfus in interviews and personal correspondence. By no means an original thinker where race and ethnicity were concerned, Huysmans blamed the Jews for the numerous financial scandals that had recently erupted in France, holding Jewish bankers responsible for the country's moral and economic woes. Although many distinguished French intellectuals, including Émile Zola, Charles Péguy, Anatole France and Marcel Proust took Dreyfus' side, Huysmans dismissed the dreyfusards as rabble ('de la racaille').[5]

Huysmans' disenchantment, both personal and artistic, with Zola led him to question his former mentor's motives in championing Dreyfus. He claimed that Zola had defended Dreyfus merely as a publicity stunt in order to draw attention to his latest novel. When Zola suddenly died as the result of a blocked chimney flue in September 1902, Huysmans was ambivalent. Though for some years he had distanced himself from his old mentor, he told Céard, who had remained loyal to Zola, that he was saddened by the famous writer's death. He did not attend the funeral, however, claiming he feared it would disintegrate into a political uprising. But his letters to Prins indicate that he was disillusioned with the great naturalist, not only because of Zola's style of writing, which he disliked, but because of his personal life. Soon after Zola's death, Huysmans remarked sarcastically that it was fortunate the great writer had died when he did, as the expense of maintaining two households would soon have left him bankrupt. This was a reference to Zola having both a wife and a mistress who had borne him two children. Huysmans had made negative remarks more than once about Zola's adulterous relationship, which he saw as self-indulgent and immoral. His disapproval may also have been due in part to loyalty to Mme Zola, who years earlier had welcomed him and other youthful members of the naturalist group at the Médan home. Despite all that Zola had endured as a result of defending Dreyfus, Huysmans refused to believe that his old master had taken up Dreyfus' cause for any reason other than personal gain:

> Zola has thrown himself into this affair, acting like he was Hugo, to generate publicity for himself. He had no documents in hand, nor any proof. The pride of this man is so great that he told a friend of mine who had said 'We would be happy to be on your side, but have you any evidence at all [of Dreyfus' innocence]?' And he replied, 'No, but since I am Zola and I say that he is innocent, that should suffice.' This is crazy![6]

In December 1902 Huysmans sent the manuscript of *L'Oblat* off to the printer. He had written the long, and at times didactic, novel in just a little over a year. A deep admiration for the Trappists and Benedictines is apparent in the book, which many readers recognized as partly autobiographical. Once again, as in *Là-bas*, *En route* and *La Cathédrale*, Durtal was the main character. One of Huysmans' main purposes in writing *L'Oblat* was to depict the devout and self-effacing lives of Benedictine monks at a time when monastic orders were being forced to leave France. His novel was an attempt at preserving and celebrating the traditional ways of the Order in case the monks never returned. Another of his goals was to criticize the French government's anticlerical stance, especially the Laws of Association, which imposed impossible restrictions on religious groups, including the Jesuits and Benedictines. In addition to lambasting the Laws of Association and President Loubet, who implemented them, Huysmans roundly excoriated Catholic laity, priests and even the pope for failing to resist the new laws. He also wanted to describe and extol the Catholic liturgy, and to detail the history of religious hermits and oblates, dating back to the Middle Ages. Finally, Huysmans wished to reveal to his readers the beauty of medieval religious painting and sculpture. Thus, in writing this book, he had clear political and religious aims.

Having endured the flurry of attacks waged by critics on *En route* and *La Cathédrale*, Huysmans expected fury in all camps when *L'Oblat* appeared in bookshops in early 1903; he knew the book would irritate Catholic reviewers because of negative comments about the Catholic clergy, such as:

The Bishops are not worth talking about; except for the old ones, who got their promotion in better times, nearly all have been tamed and have had their claws trimmed by the Ministry of Public Worship.[7] As for the clergy, it either leans towards rationalism, or else shows shocking ignorance and listlessness. The truth is that the clergy is the product of methods that are utterly out of date.[8]

He worried that his comments about the failings of the Catholic clergy would result in another denunciation to the Index, as had happened with *La Cathédrale*, though those accusations had not resulted in any action to censure the novel. While there were some unenthusiastic reviews of *L'Oblat* by secular writers, they mostly concerned its obscure content and rambling style. Many readers found it difficult to follow. Even Prins, one of Huysmans' close friends, commented privately that the work was unreadable. The prevailing opinion of critics over the years since *L'Oblat* was published is that it is not one of Huysmans' best efforts, but nonetheless it is a useful window into his feelings and concerns during the period after he left Ligugé as well as his time as an oblate.

While *L'Oblat* draws on Huysmans' life as an oblate and includes images and characters based on his stay at Ligugé, the setting is transposed to an imaginary monastery in the Burgundy region, near Dijon, where Durtal has come to make a spiritual retreat. The monks are portrayed as pious and kind; despite their human frailties, they impress Durtal and he makes the commitment to become an oblate. Like Huysmans, Durtal lives in contented seclusion near the monastery and participates in its daily services and rituals. As was true of Huysmans, Durtal's life as an oblate is shattered when the monks are forced to move to Belgium. These aspects of the plot are largely autobiographical; however, in an interview, the author insisted that he and Durtal were not the same person:

> *The Oblate* is to some extent my story, or rather it is the story of an imaginary character in a milieu where I too once lived, a monastery that I loved and miss. I set my story in an old abbey that used to exist near Dijon. And the backdrop in my book is this admirable city, with its marvellous cathedral . . . I could never imagine one that is more beautiful. You may say that I should have used a different abbey as the setting – the abbey in Poitou where I myself lived? Well, no! The monastery where my novel (which is not a novel) takes place is imaginary, and yet real.[9]

This interview is revelatory, for in it Huysmans states that he and Durtal are *not* identical, and that Durtal is 'an imaginary character' who exists in an 'imaginary place'. Thus he claims that this work is not autobiographical, even if it contains autobiographical elements. He also suggests that this book is not precisely a novel, raising the question of what exactly it is, though he never offered any answer.[10]

It can be argued that a key aspect of *L'Oblat* is a philosophical discussion of the meaning and purpose of suffering. This was a subject that had long preoccupied Huysmans. It is likely that he first began to ponder it during Anna Meunier's long and painful decline, as he watched helplessly. After years of struggling to understand why a loving God could permit human beings to suffer without intervening, Huysmans had come to accept a concept first explained to him by Boullan: mystical substitution and reparation. This doctrine, which was widespread during the Middle Ages, held that pure, virtuous individuals (for example, saints) can choose to take upon themselves the sins of others and make reparation by suffering in their stead. Suffering should, according to this doctrine, be welcomed and joyfully endured, for it is redemptive. Huysmans had already discussed this belief in *En route* and in his biography of St Lydwina, but he explored it further in *L'Oblat*, depicting Durtal first learning about and then embracing it. Towards the end of Huysmans' life, as he lay dying of cancer, he took comfort in the belief that through his suffering he was atoning for his own sins and those of others.[11]

Although it is a lengthy book that covers a confusing variety of topics, *L'Oblat* contains a number of deeply moving passages based on Huysmans' own experiences at Ligugé. Perhaps the most powerful passage of *L'Oblat* depicts the Benedictine monks' departure for Belgium and the abbot's farewell, seen through Durtal's eyes:

'Good-bye my children,' said [the abbot] in the doorway of the compartment, as he shook hands with Durtal and M. Lampre. 'Courage! Be brave! We shall meet again!'

Huysmans at home at Maison Notre Dame, at Ligugé, 1900. (Photo by Léon Leclaire, his close friend.)

As the train started, they knelt down on the platform and for the last time he blessed them, making a big sign of the Cross. Then, in clouds of steam and to the clatter of rolling wheels, all were gone.[12]

L'Oblat ends with Durtal's plaintive prayer, chiding God for allowing him to falsely believe that he could live happily for the rest of his days as an oblate:

The experiment is over; Val-des-Saints is dead; I assisted at the internment of the monastery, and even played the part of sexton in helping to dig the grave of its Office. This is the sum-total of my doings as an oblate, and I am no longer one, for I have been torn away from my cloister.

O God Almighty, I fear it is rather naughty of me to say so, but, really, my faith in Thee is somewhat shaken. It looked as if Thou were guiding me to a haven of safety. After many hardships at last I reach it; I take a chair to sit down for a rest and, behold, crack goes the chair, and I am landed on the floor.

I am wondering now whether the same dishonesty prevails in the Heavenly workshops as in the earthly ones? Whether the celestial cabinet-makers also manufacture cheap and nasty chairs, the legs of which give way as soon as you sit on them?[13]

At the end of his prayer, which is also the conclusion of the novel, Durtal begs God to help him begin a new life, 'no matter where, so long as it is far from ourselves, and close unto Thee'[14] ('n'importe où, pourvu que ce soit loin de nous-mêmes et près de Vous!').[15]

Like Durtal in *L'Oblat*, Huysmans strove to conquer his self-absorption and tendency to overanalyse his thoughts and feelings. But as he settled into life in Paris, there were many temptations and distractions. Although he claimed to have sworn off women after his conversion and oblature, Huysmans was never really free of sexual desires. His youth as a libertine was not so easily forgotten. No matter how resolutely he tried to keep 'petticoats' ('les jupons') out of his life, he continued to have equivocal relationships shortly before and soon after becoming an oblate. His unpleasant experience with La Sol had made him determined to avoid all women – except nuns. However, this vow proved to be impossible for him to keep. Perhaps the most intense of these late-in-life relationships began in 1899, when a naive young woman of noble descent named Henriette du Fresnel wrote to him after reading *En route*, seeking spiritual guidance. It all began innocently enough: Henriette wanted to become a nun, but her family was strongly opposed to the idea. Huysmans sympathized with her and wrote words of encouragement. Their correspondence continued for two years, until eventually she asked to meet with him. He acquiesced. In 1901, when she was 22, they met for the first time, and she soon began visiting him regularly at his apartment, unaccompanied and unbeknown to her parents. The society of the time frowned on such meetings, and Huysmans knew that she was lying to her family about her whereabouts. He was well aware of the danger, both to her reputation and his own, but did nothing to prevent her from coming to see him, often for hours at a time. He gave her the affectionate nickname 'the little bird' ('le petit oiseau'), telling

Prins and others that she was both charming and bothersome, and claiming that there was nothing inappropriate about their friendship, despite appearances to the contrary. At first Henriette assured Huysmans that she loved him purely as a daughter might her father, but in late 1903, she wrote him a passionate love letter. He confided to Prins:

> The little bird finally wrote me a letter telling me that I was not mistaken, that when she spoke to me of daughterly love, she was really feeling a different kind of love! When she came, I asked her if she was crazy, and I told her once again that I couldn't love her except like an elderly uncle loves his young niece, and that I was far too old to get married, etc.[16]

For all his protestations that he did not love Henriette, Huysmans clearly found her delightful and attractive. Although he had taken the vows of a Benedictine oblate, he evidently saw nothing wrong with receiving her at his flat, even after her declaration of love, and he continued to insist that he had no deep feelings for her. Eventually, her family found out about the situation and sent her off to visit relatives in England, but this did nothing to cool her ardour; he told Prins:

> I received wild letters. She came back, and seeing where things were headed, I had to tell her, as decently as possible, about the mechanisms of love. I was hoping to disgust her. But she simply answered that she belonged to me, and that 'she was only my little bird'. I was really perturbed, as you can imagine. So I told her I was almost 57 and she was 24, and that it was ridiculous. All of a sudden, she got angry and told me she didn't care about age, and that she loved me just as I was. In short, if nothing happened between us it's because I used a good amount of willpower. Her mother came to see me, and all I could say to her was 'what do you want me to do? I've done nothing to attract her to my place; I haven't even flirted with her, and I didn't take her when she offered herself.'[17]

One may wonder how Huysmans could have believed he had done nothing to encourage the young woman, since he had met privately with her in his flat for lengthy visits on many occasions. In December 1904 he revealed to Leclaire that he had embraced and passionately kissed her, but had later regretted it: 'Things have heated up. The little bird was here and she was complaining, saying "Who else loves you the way I do? I want you to love me, and me alone . . ." It all ended stupidly, in each other's arms, in a frenzy of kisses.'[18]

It is easy to imagine the frustration of Henriette's mother, who had hoped to see her daughter happily married to a young man of her aristocratic class. But apparently she did not accuse Huysmans of improper behaviour, and both writer and mother agreed that there was not much to be done with such a headstrong girl. It is hard not to sympathize with Henriette, who at this point had been visiting Huysmans (according to a letter he wrote to Prins) twice a month for four years, and who hoped for a more lasting commitment from him – likely marriage. The closeness of their relationship is evident in an incident that occurred in 1906, the year before Huysmans' death, when he was already very ill. He was rushed to a medical clinic so suddenly that even his housekeeper had no idea where he had been taken. When Henriette heard of the emergency, she searched for him for hours, stopping at numerous clinics before she finally found the right one and rushed to his bedside. Although Huysmans had other complicated relationships with women during the last years of his life, including a flirtation with the writer Myriam Harry, 'the little bird' was the woman he cared for most. In part he was attracted to her because she was deeply religious, but he also appreciated her feminine charms, affectionate nature and literary talent, remarking that she had written a prose poem that showed considerable ability.[19] As we shall see, the two continued their close friendship until his death.

The last good year of Huysmans' life was 1904. As such, it merits our attention, for it was rich and productive. During that year he continued his 'platonic liaison', as he put it, with Henriette du Fresnel. This relationship brought him affection

and brightened his otherwise rather sombre life. His health at
this point was fairly good, although he periodically complained of
toothache and jaw pain. His doctors and dentists were unaware
that these were symptoms of oral cancer, likely caused by heavy
smoking. They attributed his discomfort to rheumatism, neuralgia
and misaligned teeth, and treated him accordingly. He had no idea
these problems were much more than a passing aggravation. The
year saw several new publications: a new preface to *À rebours*
marking the novel's twentieth anniversary, and a glowing
foreword to a posthumous collection of Verlaine's religious poetry.
The foreword was his determined attempt to rehabilitate Paul
Verlaine, whose reputation as a drunkard and homosexual had led
the general public to ignore his conversion to Catholicism late in
life and the deeply spiritual poetry it inspired. The year 1904 also
saw the publication of *Trois primitifs*, a study of paintings that he
had observed and admired in German museums.

As always, he was restless. He had grown dissatisfied with his
apartment on rue de Babylone and abruptly resolved to move once
again, complaining that his neighbours were unbearably noisy:
'Can you imagine that two old bitches upstairs trundle furniture
around and drag beds during the night – right above my head! It's
impossible to sleep . . . I was starting to develop a nervous disorder
after such nights, so I had to give notice!'[20]

His new, luxurious apartment was in a handsome building at
31 rue Saint-Placide, not far from his beloved church of Saint-
Sulpice. The flat was expensive, but he was delighted with it,
declaring that it was the most elegant place he had ever lived in.
It was also to be his last.

After the move, Huysmans settled into a pleasant routine
marked by frequent visits to the churches of the Latin Quarter
and get-togethers with friends, including an old companion
from his untamed youth, the painter Jean-Louis Forain, who
had recently become a devout Catholic after years of carousing.
There were also occasional meetings of the Académie Goncourt,
over which he presided, though he looked forward to the end
of his term later that year. But 1904 was not without unpleasant

Session of the Académie Goncourt (in Paris at Léon Hennique's home) in 1903: left to right, Lucien Descaves, Gustave Geffroy, Rosny elder, Joris-Karl Huysmans, Léon Hennique, Léon Daudet, Rosny younger and Élémir Bourges.

surprises. Suddenly, in the spring, he fell ill with a malady that was diagnosed as influenza and spent weeks sequestered in his apartment, languishing in bed. 'This filthy malady is just like being poisoned,' he fumed. 'One drags along without getting over it' ('C'est un véritable empoisonnement que cette cochonnerie de maladie-là! – on traîne avec, sans arriver à se guérir').[21] It became evident that Huysmans was frail and susceptible to infections. This may have been the result of the undiagnosed cancer that was undermining his strength.

In early autumn he felt well enough to travel to Lourdes, where he visited the Leclaires and explored the city. Though the ugly architecture of Lourdes horrified him, of particular interest was the famous shrine, along with the throngs of pilgrims and the stories of many miracles that had reportedly occurred there. He took notes on all that he saw and resolved to write a book set in this famous city. Lourdes intrigued, disgusted and inspired him. Its bizarre mix of medieval art and modern religious kitsch, and the 'admirable and ignoble' examples of humanity among the tens of thousands of people from around the world, captured his imagination. He made a careful study of a number of miraculous cures, forcing himself to consider the possibility that some were likely spurious. Ultimately, because he was himself a believer in miracles, he decided that many of the reports were true, and that 'Concerning miraculous cures, there are unheard of things . . . One is plunged into the incomprehensible' ('Au point de vue des guérisons miraculeuses, il y a des choses inouïes . . . On est dans l'inintelligible').[22] After several more visits to Lourdes, he began to write the work that would become *Les Foules de Lourdes*. It was not a novel but a book about the shrine. In December he convened the second Prix Goncourt awards ceremony, at which the winner, novelist Léon Frapié, was honoured. Huysmans had supported Frapié, whose work is now virtually forgotten. As 1904 came to a close, he wished Prins a happy and healthy new year, adding 'C'est si précieux la santé!' ('Health is such a precious thing!').[23] He was soon to learn the full import of this statement.

As the new year 1905 began, Huysmans' state of health seemed stable. Though still suffering from pain in his teeth and jaw, he was busy writing *Les Foules de Lourdes* and was involved in activities tied to his status as a famous writer, giving interviews to newspapers and magazines and conferring with Stock, his publisher. Confident that he would soon complete his book about Lourdes, he was anticipating correcting the proofs and the inevitable battle between Catholic and secular literary critics that was sure to ensue when the book was published. Because he had made no effort to distance himself from Henriette, his relationship with her grew ever more tumultuous. The young woman made no secret of her sexual attraction to him. Though he continued to find her rather bothersome, he admitted to Prins that he was drawn to her and that there was nothing that could be done about the situation: 'My little bird is still fluttering about the house. What a strange little being! She never tires of it, but it's sometimes quite annoying to have a little girl who is twirling around you and kissing you – when you don't want to go any further!'[24] He still believed that he had done nothing to encourage her and that he merely wanted to help her pursue a religious vocation.

Clearly, Huysmans was not being honest with himself. In a letter to Leclaire, he revealed that he feared falling into the 'abyss' ('le gouffre'). If they became lovers, he felt, it would mean her ruination, for he had no intention of marrying her – or anyone else. But it was far too late to end the relationship, so he resolved to continue urging her to become a nun. In a private diary in 1905, he expressed his torment:

> I did not attract this child. I wanted to help her enter a convent. Is this the result? I'm devoured by filthy thoughts, haunted by her and at times I'm overcome by vertigo and obsession. There is no way out of this. What will happen . . . if she doesn't enter the convent? I forced her to write to the abbess. What a new cross to bear.[25]

Huysmans continued working on *Les Foules de Lourdes* and tried to cope with Henriette's conflicting desires to become either his lover

Saint-Martin Abbey at Ligugé.

Huysmans at Ligugé, 1904, photographed by Léon Leclaire.

or a nun. He took her side when she told her family she wanted to enter a Benedictine convent, but she then changed her mind, probably because of her interest in him.

His life changed abruptly for the worse in October 1905, when he was stricken with a particularly virulent form of shingles that left him temporarily blind, forced to rely on his secretary Jean de Caldain for help with daily tasks. While it is not clear if this illness was aggravated by the cancer that was developing in his mouth and jaw, it marked the beginning of a long period of suffering that was to end only in death. Yet even as he lay for months in a darkened room, the will to communicate prevailed over his pain, and he dictated a flood of letters to his friends. A note he sent to Prins after two months in bed makes clear the extent of his misery:

> My dear friend, the situation drags on and on. I'm still confined to bed, unable to read or write. My suffering has not much improved.
>
> I wish you and your family good health, dear friend, for it's truly awful to be without it. Unfortunately, I'm in a good position to know what that's like.[26]

The two months of misery became three, then four and finally five. It was now 1906. Huysmans had lost nearly half a year and was unable to work or even to engage in normal activities. At last, in late April, after undergoing three operations, he regained his vision. By May he was finally able to correct the proofs of *Les Foules de Lourdes*. This work, his last, was published later that year. It sold well and he was pleased with the reviews. The book is a sort of essay expressing Huysmans' opinions about Lourdes, miracles and mysticism.

While he was now able to see, his other problems – headaches, jaw pain and ulcers on his neck – worsened. Doctors put Huysmans through a variety of often painful treatments, including the extraction of most of his teeth, and X-rays (both blue and green, as he told friends). When all else failed, they recommended he go to the south of France, where it was hoped that the fresh air and sunshine might help cure him. Perhaps suspecting that he did not have much longer to live, Huysmans decided to make a sentimental visit to the Trappist monastery of Notre-Dame d'Igny, where years earlier he had returned to the Catholic faith. Despite poor health, he was overjoyed to be back in this beloved monastic retreat where he had had such a powerful religious experience. Most of all, he delighted in the natural beauty of the place, in its ponds, forests and living creatures. God's presence was palpable. He wrote happily to the Abbé Mugnier:

Huysmans' tombstone at Montparnasse Cemetery, Paris.

I'm swept away by nature, by the water . . . I'm in love with it. The pond is marvellous, criss-crossed by dragonflies – especially baby dragonflies: little winged tubes that seem made of liquid turquoise! . . . This whole world is throbbing with life. It absorbs the sky and the trees, drinking up all the reflections! And I was able to smoke cigarettes on the shore of the pond. At last my body feels almost right again and my soul is almost joyous.[27]

The final year of Huysmans' life was darkened by intense suffering. His cancer had at last been diagnosed, but all attempts at slowing the disease, including operations on his jaw and neck, failed. He made a will and began to go through his manuscripts and correspondence, ordering Jean de Caldain to destroy many personal documents, including his correspondence with Anna Meunier. Caldain secretly preserved certain manuscripts, but much valuable material was lost. Huysmans steadfastly believed that through his suffering he was expiating his sins and those of others. In a letter to the writer Myriam Harry, he remarked sadly: 'I have a vague intuition that henceforth I shall be led out of the paths of literature and into the expiatory ways of suffering, until I come to die.'[28]

During the last months of his life, he was named to the Légion d'Honneur at the high rank of Officier, in recognition of his literary achievements. (His previous award of *Chevalier de la Légion d'Honneur* had been in recognition of his long career as a civil servant.) A few weeks before his death, Henriette du Fresnel, who had faithfully visited him as often as she could, entered a Benedictine convent and remained there until her death in 1941. Huysmans died on 12 May 1907 and was buried at Montparnasse Cemetery. His tomb bears the simple inscription: *J.-K. Huysmans Président de l'Académie Goncourt.* The Abbé Mugnier presided over the funeral mass at Notre-Dame-des-Champs. A large crowd followed the funeral cortège.

Epilogue

For well over a century J.-K. Huysmans has intrigued readers with his often ironic insights into the minds and souls of his protagonists. Of great interest as well is his idiosyncratic style, seasoned with neologisms, technical terms, religious expressions and slang. There can be no doubt that Huysmans is a major French writer, though not so well known as his one-time mentor Émile Zola, or his lifelong idol Charles Baudelaire. With the recent publication of his complete novels in the Bibliothèque de la Pléiade by Éditions Gallimard, a prestigious French series that selects authors whose works are deemed to be enduring classics, he has entered the literary canon, joining the likes of Voltaire, Baudelaire, Zola and Proust.[1]

Part of his appeal can be explained by the characters he portrays, all of whom are lonely, troubled individuals who long to escape from the dullness of everyday existence. His protagonists, like Huysmans himself, are profoundly dissatisfied with life, searching for some form of transcendence, whether through art, sensual pleasure or religion. Huysmans expresses a disquiet that is also inherent in our post-modern age.

It is fitting to review Huysmans' life along with his work, since the two are intertwined. Trapped in a tedious, ill-paying civil service job for decades, beset by bouts of neuralgia, anxiety and indigestion, he yearned to flee from reality, or at least to isolate himself in a safe haven. The solitude he sought proved difficult to find, especially after he achieved notoriety at the age of 36 with the publication of *À rebours* in 1884. From that time on he was in the public eye, though it was his later novels *En route* and *La Cathédrale* that made him a celebrity, pursued by journalists and enthusiastic fans. Despite his complaints that his books were too often attacked by critics, he was selected for high honours. During his lifetime he received two awards from the Légion d'Honneur: the first for his work as a long-time government employee, the second for his achievements as a writer. Though he was never rich, he eventually attained a comfortable lifestyle thanks to his salary at the Ministry of the Interior, along with the royalties from his books. In spite of his failure to find a lasting spiritual refuge where he could feel sheltered from the outside world and commit himself to prayer and writing, he seems to have at last achieved a sort of inner peace through his religious faith. Though his final days were painful, he died a devout Catholic, in the company of close friends and mourned by an admiring public.

Huysmans was a man of prejudices and contradictions: he made misogynistic comments in his novels and correspondence but was a devoted companion to Anna Meunier for twenty years, and a loving, if unsettling, friend to Henriette du Fresnel; in addition, he praised and supported the work of several female writers, including Myriam Harry and Rachilde (the pen name of Marguerite Vallette-Eymery). There were other contradictions: though he had sympathy for the poor and the downtrodden, he was also frequently repulsed by them; and while he certainly felt pity for victims of injustice, he sided with the antidreyfusards in the Dreyfus Affair – even after Dreyfus' innocence had been demonstrated – because he disliked and distrusted Jews. This antisemitism is one of the more troubling aspects of his personality, and evidence of it can be found in his writings.[2] His prejudices did not end there; he also disliked the people of southern France, who, he maintained, were not really French at all, but an inferior race. Finally, given his level of education and sceptical nature, Huysmans' utter credulity concerning black magic and the occult seems surprising, but belief in the occult was widespread in the late nineteenth century, and, after doctors failed to cure Anna Meunier, Huysmans lost faith in science. The mysterious events that sometimes occur in the midst of everyday life interested him greatly, and in an effort to keep an open mind to such phenomena, he sometimes drifted into the realm of superstition.

Despite his personal failings, Huysmans was a faithful and generous friend who gave money to writers in financial difficulty, including Verlaine, and assisted the families of deceased colleagues. Along with Mallarmé, he was the executor of Villiers de l'Isle-Adam's will; the two men took time away from their own work to prepare the manuscript of Villiers' play *Axël* so that it could be published and the proceeds go to his widow and child. Huysmans and Mallarmé had paid many of Villiers' final expenses and, when their funds ran out, Huysmans appealed to *Le Figaro*'s editor, who gave them the money to bury him.

Huysmans leaves a lasting literary legacy. A whole generation of young symbolist and decadent writers were influenced by his novels, particularly *À rebours*, as were several youthful British and Irish writers of the time, including Oscar Wilde, George Moore and Arthur Symons. The surrealists, including André Breton, admired him and found his novel *En rade*, with its illogical dream sequences, especially inspiring. Breton believed that Huysmans' novels had opened the way to the expression of a modern artistic sensibility.

His influence goes beyond the late nineteenth- and early twentieth-century period. A noteworthy example is the contemporary French author Michel Houellebecq, whose novel *Soumission* (Submission), published in 2015, depicts a world-weary Sorbonne professor who specializes in Huysmans and attempts to emulate him by making a retreat at the monastery in Ligugé, where Huysmans became an oblate. Unlike Huysmans, the cynical protagonist, François, fails to find spiritual solace. He is a satirical persona of Houellebecq, just as Durtal is an ironic alter ego of Huysmans. Houellebecq – who is, as was Huysmans, a highly controversial writer – has said, 'I think he [Huysmans] could be a real friend to me,' adding, 'He lets the reader stay one step ahead of him, inviting us to laugh at him, and his overly plaintive, awful, or ludicrous descriptions, even before he laughs at himself.'[3] Another modern example of Huysmans' influence is the punk musician and writer Richard Hell, who attests to having been profoundly affected by *À rebours*, a book that he considers the 'primary source' of his own art, the essence of which is 'making your own world'.[4]

Huysmans constantly strove to expand the limits of the novel as a form. Perhaps his most enduring literary contribution will prove to be his many experiments with the overlapping genres of autobiography and fiction. Surely there was also a compelling personal motivation behind this experimentation. Perhaps merging aspects of his own life with imagined experiences allowed him both to discover more about himself and to escape himself by creating a new, evolving fictional identity.

References

All translations from the French are by the author, unless otherwise stated.

1 Beginnings

1 Robert Baldick, *The Life of J.-K. Huysmans*, foreword and additional notes by Brendan King (Sawtry, 2006). Despite its over-reliance on Huysmans' fiction as a source of information about his life, this book contains a wealth of meticulously researched material that is most valuable to scholars, including the author of this study.
2 Christopher Lloyd, *J.-K. Huysmans and the Fin-de-Siècle Novel* (Edinburgh, 1990), p. 3.
3 Jean-Marie Seillan, *Joris-Karl Huysmans: Interviews* (Paris, 2002), p. 418.
4 Baldick, *The Life of J.-K. Huysmans*, p. 5.
5 Henry Céard and Jean de Caldain, *Huysmans intime* (Paris, 1957), p. 70.
6 Ibid.
7 Seillan, *Huysmans: Interviews*, p. 146.
8 See Céard and Caldain, *Huysmans intime*, pp. 74–5.
9 Baldick, *The Life of J.-K. Huysmans*, p. 51.
10 For information on Ludo, see Jean Jacquinot, 'Un ami de Huysmans: Ludovic de Francmesnil (1852–1930)', *Bulletin de la Société J.-K. Huysmans*, 24 (1952), pp. 220–24, p. 222.
11 Céard and Caldain, *Huysmans intime*, p. 117. (It should be mentioned that Céard's recollections, written years after the events he describes, are not always accurate.)
12 J.-K. Huysmans, *Marthe*, trans. Brendan King (Sawtry, 2006), p. 118.

2 Under the Influence of Zola and Naturalism

1 Henry Brandreth, *Huysmans* (New York, 1963), p. 23.
2 J.-K. Huysmans, *The Vatard Sisters*, trans. Brendan King (Sawtry, 2012), pp. 71–2.
3 For a study of this theme in Huysmans' works, see Ruth Antosh, *Reality and Illusion in the Novels of J.-K. Huysmans* (Amsterdam, 1986). See also Victor Brombert, *The Romantic Prison: The French Tradition* (Princeton, NJ, 2015).
4 King, trans., *Vatard Sisters*, p. 123.
5 Ibid., p. 88.
6 J.-K. Huysmans, *Lettres à Theodore Hannon (1876–1886)*, ed. Pierre Cogny and Christian Berg (Saint-Cyr-Sur-Loire, 1985), p. 105.
7 J.-K. Huysmans, *Lettres inédites à Edmond de Goncourt*, ed. Pierre Lambert (Paris, 1956), p. 54, n. 1.
8 J. W. Sandiford-Pellé, trans., *Living Together* (London, 1969), p. 200.
9 Ibid., p. 75.
10 Anna had lived in Paris during the Prussian siege. The novel was never completed; the manuscript was likely destroyed by Huysmans shortly before his death.
11 J.-K. Huysmans, *Drifting*, trans. Brendan King (Sawtry, 2018), p. 87.
12 Huysmans, *Lettrés à Hannon*, p. 231.
13 Barbara Beaumont, *The Road from Decadence: From Brothel to Cloister. Selected Letters of J.-K. Huysmans* (London, 1989), p. 40.
14 Ibid.
15 Ibid., p. 70.
16 Ibid., p. 44.

3 *À rebours* and Beyond

1 J.-K. Huysmans, *Against Nature*, trans. Robert Baldick (New York, 1977), p. 35.
2 Ibid., p. 36.
3 Ibid.
4 Ibid., pp. 67–8.
5 Ibid., p. 40.
6 J.-K. Huysmans, *Lettres inédites à Émile Zola*, ed. Pierre Lambert (Geneva, 1953), pp. 106–7, n. 1.

7 Barbara Beaumont, *The Road from Decadence: From Brothel to Cloister. Selected Letters of J.-K. Huysmans* (London, 1989), p. 55.
8 Ibid.
9 J.-K. Huysmans, *Lettres inédites à Camille Lemonnier*, ed. Gustave Vanwelkenhuyzen (Geneva, 1957), p. 112, n. 1.
10 Ibid., p. 111.
11 Beaumont, *Road from Decadence*, p. 56.
12 Jean Jacquinot, 'Louis-Alexis Orsat, un ami "perdu et retrouvé" de J.-K. Huysmans', *Bulletin de la Société J.-K. Huysmans*, 23 (1951), pp. 165–76, p. 173.
13 Robert Baldick, *The Life of J.-K. Huysmans*, foreword and additional notes by Brendan King (Sawtry, 2006), p. 144.
14 Beaumont, *Road from Decadence*, pp. 68–9.
15 Ibid., p. 69.
16 Huysmans, *Lettres à Zola*, p. 121.
17 J.-K. Huysmans, *Stranded (En rade)*, trans. Brendan King (Sawtry, 2010), p. 49.
18 Anna's illness manifested itself in neurological symptoms such as temporary paralysis, along with gradually increasing mental illness. Her frightening symptoms puzzled doctors at the time, but it now seems plausible that they were caused by late-stage syphilis.
19 For a discussion of Huysmans' interest in dreams, see King's Introduction to *Stranded*, pp. 10–13.
20 King, trans., *Stranded*, pp. 9–10.
21 J.-K. Huysmans, *Lettres inédites à Arij Prins: 1885–1907*, ed. Louis Gillet (Geneva, 1977), p. 42.
22 Ibid., p. 34.
23 Huysmans often referred to Anna as 'my wife', though they never married.
24 Huysmans, *Lettres à Prins*, p. 70.
25 Ibid.
26 Ibid., p. 73.
27 Beaumont, *Road from Decadence*, p. 74.

4 Descending into Darkness: *Là-bas*, the Abbé Boullan and the Occult

1 Édouard Dujardin, 'Huysmans et *La Revue indépendante*', *Le Figaro*, 14 May 1927.
2 Daniel Habrekorn, ed., *Correspondance à trois: Bloy, Villiers, Huysmans* (Vanves, 1980), p. 99.

3 The Naundorffists were a group of royalist followers of Karl Naundorff, a watchmaker born in Potsdam who claimed to be Louis XVII and rightful heir to the throne of France.

4 J.-K. Huysmans, *Lettres inédites à Arij Prins: 1885–1907*, ed. Louis Gillet (Geneva, 1977), p. 156.

5 Ibid., p. 155.

6 Robert Baldick, *The Life of J.-K. Huysmans*, foreword and additional notes by Brendan King (Sawtry, 2006), p. 187.

7 Ibid., p. 226.

8 J.-K. Huysmans, *Lettres inédites à Jules Destrée*, ed. Gustave Vanwelkenhuyzen (Geneva, 1967), p. 167.

9 The 'Cahier rose' is a journal in which Boullan confessed his sins. A typed copy is in the Fonds Lambert, No. 95, at the Bibliothèque de l'Arsenal in Paris.

10 For a discussion of the relationship between Huysmans and Boullan, see Joanny Bricaud, *J.-K. Huysmans et le satanisme* (Paris, 1912).

11 Gilles de Rais (1404–1440) was a French nobleman who served in Joan of Arc's army. But he was also a murderous paedophile responsible for the grisly deaths of many children. He was tried for his crimes and executed.

12 J.-K. Huysmans, *Là-bas: A Journey into the Self*, trans. Brendan King (Sawtry, 1992), p. 22.

13 Ibid., p. 25.

14 J.-K. Huysmans, *Là-bas* (Paris, 1978) , p. 40.

15 King, trans., *Là-bas*, p. 21.

16 Huysmans, *Lettres à Prins*, p. 215.

17 Ibid., p. 219.

18 Ruth Antosh, 'The Role of Paintings in Three Novels by J.-K. Huysmans', *Nineteenth-Century French Studies*, XII–XIII/4 (1984), pp. 131–46.

19 Little is known about Henriette Maillat (née Picot). She was well read and knowledgeable about contemporary French poetry and fiction. Besides Huysmans, she had affairs with several other writers, including Sâr Péladan, Léon Bloy and Guy de Maupassant.

20 Maurice Belval, *Des ténèbres à la lumière: étapes de la pensée mystique de J.-K. Huysmans* (Paris, 1968), p. 127.

21 Huysmans, *Lettres à Prins*, p. 219.

22 J.-K. Huysmans, *Carnet Vert*, n.d., n.p. This is an unpublished journal in the Fonds Lambert, Bibliothèque de l'Arsenal, Paris.

23 Abbé Arthur Mugnier, *J.-K. Huysmans à La Trappe* (Paris, 1927), pp. 10–11.

24 Belval, *Des ténèbres à la lumière*, p. 126.

25 Ibid., p. 128.
26 Ibid., p. 130.
27 Ibid., p. 131.

5 The Spiritual Journey Begins: Religious Retreats
and Huysmans' Conversion

1   Barbara Beaumont, ed. and trans., *The Road from Decadence: From
    Brothel to Cloister. Selected Letters of J.-K. Huysmans* (London, 1989),
    p. 107.
2   Ibid., p. 113.
3   Ibid., pp. 113–14.
4   Henceforth in this chapter, we will refer to this novel as *En route*; this
    was the book's title when it was published. Huysmans' decision to
    change the title will be discussed in the next chapter.
5   J.-K. Huysmans, *Lettres inédites à Arij Prins*, ed. Louis Gillet (Geneva,
    1977), p. 238.
6   Ibid., p. 240.
7   Baldick assumes that *En route* is an exact account of Huysmans' own
    experience at Igny, but gives no evidence to support this assumption.
8   W. Fleming, trans., *En route* (Los Angeles, CA, 2008), pp. 131–2.
9   An oblate is a lay member of a monastery who participates in the
    services but does not take monastic vows.
10 Fleming, *En route*, pp. 151–2.
11 Pierre Cogny, ed., *Là-haut ou Notre-Dame de la Salette, suivi du journal
    d''En route'* (Paris, 1965), p. 236.
12 Robert Baldick, *The Life of J.-K. Huysmans*, foreword and additional
    notes by Brendan King (Sawtry, 2006), p. 211.
13 Cogny, *Là-haut, suivi du journal d''En route'*, p. 227.
14 Beaumont, *Road to Decadence*, p. 115.
15 The Fleming translation of the following quoted passage omits or
    changes several words and phrases of a sexual nature. My corrections
    appear in brackets.
16 Fleming, *En route*, p. 60.
17 Beaumont, *Road from Decadence*, p. 114.
18 Durtal confesses to the sin of lust – along with other sins that loom less
    large – but his sexual behaviour includes adultery and desecration of
    a host, which are described in *Là-bas* and are in all probability purely
    fictional.

19 For a description of Huysmans' ordeal during the night before he was to confess his sins, see Mugnier's comments in Abbé Arthur Mugnier, *J.-K. Huysmans à La Trappe* (Paris, 1927), p. 30.
20 Beaumont, *Road from Decadence*, p. 120.
21 Ibid., p. 121.
22 Fleming, *En route*, p. 219.
23 Beaumont, *Road from Decadence*, pp. 121–2.
24 Ibid., p. 124.

6 In Search of a Monastery: The Road to Ligugé

1 Barbara Beaumont, ed. and trans., *The Road from Decadence: From Brothel to Cloister. Selected Letters of J.-K. Huysmans* (London, 1989), p. 130.
2 Abbé Arthur Mugnier, *J.-K. Huysmans à La Trappe* (Paris, 1927).
3 Jean-Marie Seillan, *Joris-Karl Huysmans: Interviews* (Paris, 2002), p. 126.
4 Ibid., p. 128.
5 Beaumont, *Road from Decadence*, p. 130.
6 Ibid., p. 256.
7 Ibid.
8 Ibid., p. 134.
9 Ibid., p. 263.
10 Pierre Cogny, '63 lettres inédites de J.-K. Huysmans à Gustave Boucher', *Bulletin de la société J.-K. Huysmans*, 64 (1975), pp. 1–62, p. 23.
11 W. Fleming, trans., *En route* (Los Angeles, CA, 2008), p. 206.
12 J.-K. Huysmans, *Lettres inédites à Arij Prins*, ed. Louis Gillet (Geneva, 1977), p. 277.
13 Sebastian Kneipp (1821–1897) was an Austrian priest who developed a new method of water therapy that he believed cured a variety of illnesses. The Kneipp method was popular in late nineteenth-century Europe; it involved cold-water showers, baths and therapeutic massage. The Kneipp firm still exists today.
14 Cogny, '63 lettres à Boucher', pp. 29–30.
15 Huysmans, *Lettres à Prins*, p. 285.
16 J.-K. Huysmans, *The Cathedral*, trans. Clara Bell and Brendan King (Sawtry, 2011), p. 123.
17 Ibid., p. 34.
18 Huysmans, *Lettres à Prins*, p. 298.

19 Guy Chastel, *J.-K. Huysmans et ses amis* (Paris, 1957), p. 54.
20 Cogny, '63 lettres à Boucher', pp. 13–14.
21 Huysmans, *Lettres à Prins*, pp. 326–7.
22 Octave Uzanne, 'Quelques heures à la Maison Notre-Dame', *Écho de Paris*, www.huysmans.org, 21 September 1900.
23 Ibid.
24 Huysmans, *Lettres à Prins*, p. 325.
25 Ibid.
26 Ibid., pp. 323–4.
27 Ibid., p. 328.
28 Uzanne, 'Quelques heures'.
29 Edmond de Goncourt's will had provided funds to establish the now famous Académie Goncourt, charged with awarding a prize to one author each year, which had named Huysmans as its first president.
30 Huysmans, *Lettres à Prins*, p. 344.

7 The Final Years

1 J.-K. Huysmans, *Lettres inédites à Arij Prins*, ed. Louis Gillet (Geneva, 1977), p. 357.
2 Ibid., p. 360.
3 Ibid., p. 313.
4 Alfred Dreyfus (1859–1935) was a French army officer accused of giving military secrets to the Germans. An antisemitic superior targeted him as a traitor. In 1894 he was tried, convicted and sentenced to imprisonment on Devil's Island, off the coast of South America. It was later discovered that another officer, Charles-Marie Esterhazy, was a spy for the Germans and had actually committed the crime. Despite compelling evidence of Esterhazy's guilt, Dreyfus was convicted a second time. Émile Zola argued vehemently for Dreyfus' acquittal in a series of articles, the most famous of which, 'J'accuse', named a number of high-ranking government officials who had obstructed justice. As a result of his article, Zola was tried, found guilty of libel and sentenced to prison but fled to England, returning a year later when the charges against him were dropped. Years later, in 1906, Dreyfus was finally declared innocent and reinstated in the military.

5 For a detailed analysis of Huysmans' antisemitism, see Jean-Marie Seillan, 'Huysmans, un antisémite fin-de-siècle', *Romantisme*, 95 (1997), pp. 113–26.

6 Huysmans, *Lettres à Prins*, p. 313.

7 Perceval has mistranslated here; the true meaning is 'emasculated' or 'castrated'.

8 J.-K. Huysmans, *The Oblate of St Benedict*, trans. Edward Perceval (Sawtry, 1996), p. 264.

9 Jean-Marie Seillan, *Joris-Karl Huysmans: Interviews* (Paris, 2002), p. 366.

10 Huysmans had expressed his disillusionment with the novel as a genre that was no longer evolving.

11 For a detailed discussion of Huysmans' belief in the doctrine of mystical substitution and reparation, see Robert Baldick, *The Life of J.-K. Huysmans*, foreword and additional notes by Brendan King (Sawtry, 2006), pp. 428–30. See also Robert Ziegler, 'The Dolorist Aesthetic of J.-K. Huysmans', *Romance Quarterly*, L (April 2010), pp. 13–23.

12 Perceval, trans., *The Oblate*, p. 290.

13 Ibid., p. 302.

14 Ibid., p. 304.

15 J.-K. Huysmans, *L'Oblat* (Paris, 1908), p. 378.

16 Huysmans, *Lettres à Prins*, pp. 377–8.

17 Ibid., p. 392.

18 Brendan King, 'Seducer or Seduced? J.-K. Huysmans and Myriam Harry', 2009, www.huysmans.org.

19 For a detailed account of the relationship between Henriette du Fresnel and Huysmans, see Henri Pevel, *Pour l'amour de Huysmans* (Villelongue-d'Aude, 1984).

20 Huysmans, *Lettres à Prins*, p. 382.

21 Ibid., p. 385.

22 Ibid., p. 390.

23 Ibid., p. 393.

24 Ibid., p. 395.

25 Pevel, *Pour l'amour de Huysmans*, p. 85. Pevel does not provide a source for this passage, other than to say it is from a diary. Huysmans kept numerous notebooks and journals, some of which have not been published.

26 Huysmans, *Lettres à Prins*, p. 396.

27 Lucien Descaves, *Les dernières années de J.-K. Huysmans* (Paris, 1941), p. 188.

28 Baldick, *Life of J.-K. Huysmans*, p. 470.

Epilogue

1 J.-K. Huysmans, *Romans et nouvelles* (Paris, 2019).
2 See Jean-Marie Seillan, 'Huysmans, un antisémite fin-de-siècle', *Romantisme*, 95 (1997), pp. 113–26.
3 Adam Gollner, 'What Houellebecq Learned from Huysmans', *New Yorker*, www.newyorker.org, 12 November 2015.
4 Ibid.

Bibliography

Works by Joris-Karl Huysmans
Marthe, histoire d'une fille [1876] (Paris, 1975)
'Émile Zola et *L'Assommoir*' [1877], in *En ménage* (Paris, 1927)
Les Sœurs Vatard [1879] (Paris, 1953)
En rade; Un dilemme; Croquis parisiens [1880–87] (Paris, 1976)
En ménage [1881] (Paris, 2005)
À vau-l'eau [1882] (Paris, 1956)
À rebours [1884] (Paris, 1975)
Là-bas [1891] (Paris, 1978)
En route [1895] (Paris, 1996)
La Cathédrale [1898] (Paris, 1986)
Sainte Lydwine de Schiedam [1901] (Paris, 1901)
L'Oblat (Paris, 1908)
Les Foules de Lourdes [1906] (Paris, 1958)
Carnet vert, unpublished notebook, Collection Pierre Lambert, Bibliothèque
    de l'Arsenal, Paris
Œuvres complètes, ed. Lucien Descaves (Paris, 1928)
Romans et nouvelles (Paris, 2019)

Correspondence by Joris-Karl Huysmans
Lettres inédites à Arij Prins, ed. Louis Gillet (Geneva, 1977)
Lettres inédites à Camille Lemonnier, ed. Gustave Vanwelkenhuyzen (Geneva,
    1957)
Lettres inédites à Edmond de Goncourt, ed. Pierre Lambert (Paris, 1956)
Lettres inédites à Émile Zola, ed. Pierre Lambert (Geneva, 1953)
Lettres inédites à Jules Destrée, ed. Gustave Vanwelkenhuyzen (Geneva, 1967)
Lettres à Théodore Hannon, ed. Pierre Cogny and Christian Berg (Paris, 1985)

Works by Huysmans in Translation

Baldick, Robert, trans., *Against Nature* (*À rebours*) (New York, 1977)
Bell, Clara, and Brendan King, trans., *The Cathedral* (Sawtry, 2011)
Fleming, W., trans., *En route* (Los Angeles, CA, 2008)
King, Brendan, trans., *Drifting* (*À vau-l'eau*) (Sawtry, 2018)
—, trans., *Là-bas, A Journey into the Self* (Sawtry, 1992)
—, trans., *Marthe* (Sawtry, 2006)
—, trans., *Stranded (En rade)* (Sawtry, 2010)
—, trans., *The Vatard Sisters* (Sawtry, 2012)
Perceval, Edward, trans., *The Oblate of St Benedict* (Sawtry, 1996)
Sandiford-Pellé, J. W., trans., *Living Together* (*En ménage*) (London, 1969)

Works on Huysmans

Antosh, Ruth, *Reality and Illusion in the Novels of J.-K. Huysmans* (Amsterdam, 1986)
—, 'The Role of Paintings in Three Novels by J.-K. Huysmans', *Nineteenth-Century French Studies*, XII–XIII/4 (1984), pp. 131–46
Baldick, Robert, *The Life of J.-K. Huysmans*, foreword and additional notes by Brendan King (Sawtry, 2006)
Banks, Brian, *The Image of Huysmans* (New York, 1990)
Beaumont, Barbara, ed. and trans., *The Road from Decadence: From Brothel to Cloister. Selected Letters of J.-K. Huysmans* (London, 1989)
Belval, Maurice, *Des ténèbres à la lumière: étapes de la pensée mystique de J.-K. Huysmans* (Paris, 1968)
Brandreth, Henry R. T., *Huysmans* (New York, 1963)
Bricaud, Joanny, *J.-K. Huysmans et le satanisme* (Paris, 1912)
Brunel, Marc, and André Guyaux, *Cahier Huysmans* (Paris, 1985)
Céard, Henry, and Jean de Caldain, *Huysmans intime* (Paris, 1957)
Cogny, Pierre, *J.-K. Huysmans à la recherche de l'unité* (Paris, 1953)
—, ed., *Là-haut ou Notre-Dame de la Salette, suivi du journal d'"En route'* (Paris, 1965)
—, '63 Lettres inédites de J.-K. Huysmans à Gustave Boucher', *Bulletin de la Société J.-K. Huysmans*, 64 (1975), pp. 1–62
Coquiot, Gustave, *Le Vrai J.-K. Huysmans* (Paris, 1912)
Descaves, Lucien, *Les Dernières Années de J.-K. Huysmans* (Paris, 1941)
Dujardin, Édouard, 'Huysmans et *Le Revue indépendante*', *Le Figaro*, 14 May 1927
Dumesnil, René, *La Publication d'"En route' de J.-K. Huysmans* (Paris, 1931)
Gollner, Adam, 'What Houellebecq Learned from Huysmans', *New Yorker*, www.newyorker.com, 12 November 2015

Habrekorn, Daniel, ed., *Correspondance à trois: Bloy, Villiers, Huysmans* (Vanves, 1980)

Harry, Myriam, 'J.-K. Huysmans et Sœur Scolastica', *Le Temps*, 27 June 1932, www.huysmans.org

Issacharoff, Michael, *J.-K. Huysmans devant la critique en France (1874–1960)* (Paris, 1970)

Jacquinot, Jean, 'Louis-Alexis Orsat, un ami "perdu et retrouvé" de J.-K. Huysmans', *Bulletin de la Société J.-K. Huysmans*, 23 (1951), pp. 165–76

—, 'Un ami de Huysmans: Ludovic de Francmesnil (1852–1930)', *Bulletin de la Société J.-K. Huysmans*, 24 (1952), pp. 220–24

Kahn, Annette, *J.-K. Huysmans, Novelist, Poet, and Art Critic* (Ann Arbor, MI, 1987)

King, Brendan, 'Seducer or Seduced? J.-K. Huysmans and Myriam Harry', 2009, www.huysmans.org

Laver, James, *The First Decadent: Being the Strange Life of J.-K. Huysmans* (London, 1954)

Lefai, Henry, *Huysmans à Lourps* (Paris, 1953)

Lloyd, Christopher, *J.-K. Huysmans and the Fin-de-Siècle Novel* (Edinburgh, 1990)

Locmant, Patrice, *J.-K. Huysmans, le forçat de la vie* (Paris, 2007)

Maingon, Charles, *L'Univers artistique de J.-K. Huysmans* (Paris, 1977)

Mugnier, Abbé Arthur, *J.-K. Huysmans à La Trappe* (Paris, 1927)

Nuccitelli, Angela, 'À rebours's Symbol of the "Femme-Fleur": A Key to Des Esseintes's Obsession', *Symposium*, 28 (1974), pp. 336–44

Pevel, Henri, *Pour l'amour de Huysmans* (Villelongue-d'Aude, France, 1984)

Ridge, George Ross, *J.-K. Huysmans* (New York, 1968)

Roucan, Carine, *Le 'Roman de Durtal': une autofiction?* (Saarbrücken, 2015)

Seillan, Jean-Marie, 'Huysmans, un antisémite fin-de-siècle', *Romantisme*, 95 (1997), pp. 113–26

—, *Huysmans: politique et religion* (Paris, 2009)

—, *Joris-Karl Huysmans: Interviews* (Paris, 2002)

Smeets, Marc, *Huysmans l'inchangé: histoire d'une conversion* (Leiden, 2003)

Solal, Jérôme, *Huysmans avant Dieu* (Paris, 2010)

—, *Huysmans avec Dieu* (Paris, 2015)

Trudgian, Helen, *L'Esthétique de J.-K. Huysmans* (Paris, 1934)

Uitti, Karl D., *The Concept of Self in the Symbolist Novel* (The Hague, 1961)

Uzanne, Octave, 'Quelques heures à la Maison Notre-Dame à Ligugé', *Écho de Paris*, 21 September 1900, www.huysmans.org

Viegnes, Michel, *Le Milieu et l'individu dans la trilogie de Joris-Karl Huysmans* (Paris, 1986)

Vircondelet, Alain, *Huysmans* (Paris, 1990)

Zayed, Fernande, *Huysmans peintre de son époque (avec des documents inédits)* (Paris, 1973)

Ziegler, Robert, 'The Dolorist Aesthetic of J.-K. Huysmans', *Romance Quarterly*, L (April, 2010), pp. 13–23

General Studies of Huysmans' Period

Brombert, Victor, *The Romantic Prison: The French Tradition* (Princeton, NJ, 2015)

Griffiths, Richard, *The Reactionary Revolution: The Catholic Revival in French Literature, 1870–1914* (London, 1965)

Matthews, John H., *Surrealism and the Novel* (Ann Arbor, MI, 1966)

Porter, Laurence M., *The Literary Dream in French Romanticism: A Psychoanalytic Interpretation* (Detroit, MI, 1979)

Praz, Mario, *The Romantic Agony*, trans. Angus Davidson (Oxford, 1933)

Raimond, Michel, *La Crise du roman: des lendemains du naturalisme aux années vingt* (Paris, 1967)

Ridge, George Ross, *The Hero in French Decadent Literature* (Athens, GA, 1961)

Websites

www.huysmans.org

Acknowledgements

I wish to thank the Bibliothèque de l'Arsenal for allowing me to consult the Fonds Lambert collection of Huysmans' letters and manuscripts, and the librarians of the State University of New York at Fredonia, especially Julie Crowell. In addition, I am grateful to Vivian Constantinopoulos and Amy Salter of Reaktion Books for their help and advice, and to my inimitable assistant, Mindy Ostrander.

Photo Acknowledgements

The author and publishers wish to express their thanks to the sources listed below for illustrative material and/or permission to reproduce it. Some locations of artworks are also given below, in the interest of brevity.

AF Fotografie/Alamy Stock Photo: p. 69; Armand Hammer Museum of Art, Los Angeles: p. 45; Bibliothèque nationale de France, Paris: pp. 14, 42, 46, 53, 67; from Remy de Gourmont, *Le Livre des masques*, 3rd edn (Paris, 1896): p. 104 (photo Bibliothèque nationale de France, Paris); Musée Carnavalet, Histoire de Paris: p. 131; Musée d'Orsay, Paris: pp. 24, 49; Musée Unterlinden, Colmar: p. 64; Wikimedia Commons: pp. 9 (photo, Mu, CC 3.0), 51 (photo, Marie-Lan Nguyen, CC 4.0), 115 (photo, Danielclauzier, CC 4.0), 133 (photo, Mairie de Ligugé, CC 4.0), 136 (photo Atobar, public domain).